T0082649

# Lecture On Prayer

# Lecture On Prayer

Rev. Fred Cato Jr

iUniverse

# LECTURE ON PRAYER

*Scripture quotations from the Holy Bible, King James Version (Authorized Version). First published in 1611. Quoted from the KJV Classic Reference Bible.*

*iUniverse books may be ordered through booksellers or by contacting:*

*iUniverse*
*1663 Liberty Drive*
*Bloomington, IN 47403*
*www.iuniverse.com*
*844-349-9409*

*ISBN: 978-1-6632-3299-1 (sc)*
*ISBN: 978-1-6632-3300-4 (e)*

*Print information available on the last page.*

*iUniverse rev. date: 12/03/2021*

# Contents

Acknowledgement .................................................................vii

Introduction.........................................................................ix

Prayer is First Priority ........................................................ 1

Definition of Prayer ........................................................... 4

Type of Prayers.................................................................... 6

Power of Prayer .................................................................. 14

The Audience of Prayer ....................................................... 22

The True Audience of God.................................................... 29

Pray without Hypocrisy........................................................ 34

Unsolved Prayer .................................................................. 36

The Model Prayer ................................................................ 42

Nature and Significance of Prayer......................................... 53

The Lord's Prayer ................................................................ 56

Biblical Men and Women who prayed.................................... 58

The Prayers of the Saints (The Children of God)

    Availeth much............................................................. 101

The Lord's Prayer/The Disciples Prayer ............................... 105

Author's Note...................................................................... 111

Bibliography........................................................................ 113

# *Acknowledgement*

With gratitude, I would like to extend thanks in loving memory of my sister Rosa (Cato) Gramling who inspired me to always keep her in my prayers. Although you are gone to be with the Lord, I shall never forget your encouraging words of inspiration.

I would also love to give thanks and acknowledge my six children- four sons; James, Marshall, Jonathan, Fred III and two daughters; Brenda and Tawanda Cato. I shall always love and cherish you all. Stay prayerful and stay with the Lord, for He is our only hope for salvation. God love you all and so do I.

Lastly, I would like to acknowledge my sibling, Lillie M. Cato, William T. Cato, James L. Cato, and Rev. Benjamin L. Cato. You have been an inspiration to me in my ministry. Love you all.

# Introduction

Prayer - a person's acts of communion with God, and any other object of worship, and the words used. It is the natural result of a person's belief in God. Prayer may be individual or group, formal or spontaneous, silent or spoken. In one or more forms, it is at the center of worship. The inseparable accompaniment of sacrifice in most primitive religions, prayer occupied a central position in Jewish religion from early days. The Temple was a house of prayer, and the Psalms, or Psalter became the prayer of liturgy of the Temple and the synagogue and formed the substance of prayers in early Christianity.[i]

Christians prayer normally includes invocation, praise, thanksgiving, petition for oneself and others, confession, and appeal for forgiveness. It follows the pattern of the prayer known as the Lord's Prayer given by Jesus Christ to His disciples.[1] Prayer is understood as spiritual communion for the sake of requesting something of a deity. Prayer can be any ritual form designed to bring one into a closer relation to whatever one believes to be the ultimate. In this sense, both the dance ceremonials of the Native American and the meditation of the Buddhist seeking self-perfection are forms of prayer[2]. At the

---

[1] http://mb-soft.com/believe/txs/prayer.htm
[2] http://www.awarenessmag.com/marapr1/MA1_REFLEXIONS.HTML

highest level, sacrifice is absorbed into prayer in the sacrificial offering of self to God through total commitment. Aids to prayer evolved through the centuries, include prayer beads, which enable a worshipper to count the prayers he or she is praying; the prayer wheel, a cylindrical box containing written prayers believed to become effective as the box is revolved on its axis, used primarily by Tibetan Buddhists; and the prayer rug, used by Muslims. Prayer is communication with God. The Bible gives many general references to prayer.[3]

It tells the universal need for prayer; it prescribes prayer, it gives the name of many characters in the Bible. The scripture encourages us with numerous examples of people who asked God for a successor, and who prayed and God answered their prayers such as: Moses, Gideon, Hannah, Solomon, Hezekiah, Jehoshaphat, and to include our Lord and Savior Jesus Christ according to Saint John 17:1-26, and to include the early church according to Luke 1:13 whereas Zechariah's prayer, for a son is referred to. However, it is more likely that in his priestly function he was praying for the salvation of Israel, and the answer of God to Daniel's prayer in Daniel 9:20 came immediately through the angel Gabriel. Although Daniel's prayer was primarily for God's forgiveness and the restoration of the Jews to their land, and his initial concern for God's program for Israel caused the Lord to reveal to him an outline of Israel's future from that point on. Perhaps both prayer requests were being granted at once in an unforeseeable way.

The Bible also talks about unanswered prayers - those who pray in amiss (self-indulgent James 4:3). Those who holds on to sin in Psalm 66:18, and Proverbs 1:28. Those who despise

---

[3] http://mb-soft.com/believe/txs/prayer.htm

the law in Proverbs 28:9, those who shed innocent blood in Isaiah 1:15, those living in sin in Isaiah 59:2 and Micah 3:4, and to the stubborn in Zechariah 7:13.

Prayer is first mentioned in the Bible in Genesis 4:26. After Enos was born and named, man began to call upon the name of the Lord. Prayer is one of the most ancient expressions of religion. It is found in all times. Prayer may be a corporate or personal act utilizing various forms and techniques. Prayer has been described in its sublimity as an intimate friendship, a frequent conversation held alone with God. Each time we pray, we comes in contact with God in a profound and life changing way.

When we face hopeless situations in our relationships, businesses, work, finances, health, emotions, or children, praying to the God of hope can change the situation. When we struggle with such things as unrealized dreams, an unfulfilling life, lack of mental clarity, or emotional pain, we have access to the God who can touch every area of our lives to transform them and bring about wholeness. He wants to reach down and touch us, but first we have to reach up and touch Him in prayer. When we pray, we're saying, "I know you are real, Lord, and I want to spend time with you."

Prayer is **praising** and **worshipping** God for who He is. This takes our focus off ourselves and places it on Him. It positions Him first in our hearts and allows Him full access to our lives.

I've found that there are two sides to prayer. There is a fellowship side, and the partnership side. The **fellowship side of prayer** is when we come just to be with God in the intimacy of relationship. The **Partnership side** is when we exercise the responsibilities of partnering with Him to see the reintroduction of His rule into our circumstances. Worship, praise, adoration, and exaltation are an important part of fellowship with God, but it is also a means of partnering with Him to drive back the darkness.

When we praise God, we are saying, "Lord, you are wonderful, almighty, all powerful, the God and Creator of all things". "I exalt you above everything, and I worship you for who you are." [4]

---

[4] https://webcache.googleusercontent.com/search?q=cache:Dgo-Kg35g7oJ:
https://www.jackhayford.org/teaching/book-excerpts/the-power-of-praying-together/+&cd=2&hl=en&ct=clnk&gl=ph

# *Prayer is First Priority*

In the early church, prayer was the first priority. As we read in the Bible concern the early church, every chapter contains a triumphant shout of victory. It is a story of perpetual progress and constant victory over opposing forces and strong persecution.

As we read in *Acts 2:47: And the Lord added to the church daily such as should be saved.*

*Many of them which heard the word believed; and the number of the men was about five thousand (Acts 4:4).*

*And believers were the more added to the Lord, multitudes both of men and women (Acts 5:14).*

*And the Word of God increased; and the number of the disciples multiplied in Jerusalem greatly; and a great company of the priests were obedient to the faith (Acts 6:7).*

Now, the miracle working power of God flowed with demonstrations, signs, and wonders, as living proof of the Gospel. *And fear came upon every soul; and many wonders and signs were done by the apostles (Acts 2:43).*

*And with great power gave the apostles witness of the resurrection of the Lord Jesus and great grace was upon them all (Acts 4:33).*

*And the people with one accord gave heed unto those things which Philip spake; hearing and seeing the miracles which he did (Acts 8:6).*

*And God wrought special miracles by the hands of Paul (Acts19:11)*

The reason God's power flowed through the Early Church in such a great dimension is that the Early Church was a praying church. They did not merely pray occasionally, but *they continued steadfastly in the apostles' doctrine and fellowship, and in breaking of bread, and in prayers (Acts 2:42).*

There were three time periods designated by the Jews for public worship. The third hour of prayer was between the hours of 6:00 a.m. and 9:00 a.m. The sixth hour was between the hours of 9:00 a.m. and 12:00

noon. The ninth hour was between the hours of 12:00 noon and 3:00 p.m. During these times, believers prayed in their homes or in the temple. Peter and John were on their way to prayer when Peter saw the lame man lying at the gate of the temple. He lifted him to his feet and said: *"Silver and gold have I none; but such as I have give I thee; In the name of Jesus Christ of Nazareth rise up and walk (Acts 3:6).*

The Church of Jesus Christ was born, empowered, sustained, and overcame through prayer. Prayer was their number one priority. The disciples said, *"But we will give ourselves continually to prayer and to the ministry of the word (Acts 6:4)*

Prayer was not secondary to their ministry. It was their ministry. The disciples gave themselves to prayer. Those who were called as leaders gave themselves continually to prayer, delegating other tasks to elders and deacons. If only we could restore this apostolic order, we would experience more apostolic results.

When we look at the Early Church, we often think about the power that was so strong in Paul's life that handkerchiefs worn on his body were used as a point of contact to heal the sick and cast out demons (Acts 9:11-12). We can recall how they brought the sick and laid them on beds in the streets so Peter's shadow would fall on them, and they would be healed (Acts 5:15).

As we look more closely, we find that the power flowed through Peter, Paul, and the other apostles because they lived in an atmosphere of prayer. Through their continual prayers they engaged and defeated the powers of darkness and preached the Gospel in a demonstration of power with signs following.

When the disciples needed God's direction, they prayed. When they needed provision, they prayed. When they needed protection and deliverance they prayed. When they needed doors to open for the Gospel, they prayed. The believers prayed from house to house. They prayed in the temple, in prisons, on mountainsides, on riverbanks – wherever they went. When they faced persecution and death, they prayed in the dark, cold catacombs. Prayer was not just an occasional occurrence; it was an integral part of their lives.

# *Definition of Prayer*

Prayer is communicating with God. It is a two-way communication with God, wherein believers talk to God, and He responds through our spirit, His Word, or sometimes even in an audible voice. It takes different forms, basically, when man talks with God and God talks with man.

Prayer is described as: (1) calling upon the name of the Lord: Genesis 12:8. (2) Crying unto God: Psalms 27:7, 34:6. (3) Drawing near to God: Ps. 73:28, Hebrews 10:22. (4) Looking up to God: Ps. 5:3. (5) Lifting up souls: Ps. 25:1. (6) Lifting up the heart: Lamentations 3:41. (7) Pouring out the heart: Ps. 62:8. (8) Pouring out the soul: 1 Samuel 1:15. (9) Crying to heaven: 2 Chronicles 32:20. (10) Beseeching the Lord: Exodus 32:11. (11) Seeking God: Job 8:5. (12) Seeking the face of the Lord Ps. 27:8 and (13) Making supplication: Jeremiah 36:7.

Prayer involves not just talking to God, but it involves listening also. Prayer is communication and a one-way conversation and does not last very long. When you pray, expect God to speak to you. Most often He will do this through His written Word or by a still, small voice that seems to speak to your heart. Sometimes He will give you a vision or interpret back to your spirit what you have prayed in your heavenly prayer language.

**Prayer is telling God we Love and Adore Him.** It means coming humbly before God and speaking to Him the way we would to someone we love so dearly.

**Prayer is telling God how grateful we are:** He loved us before we were even aware that He existed. When we pray, we are saying, "I love you, Lord, and I thank you for loving me".

**Prayer is telling God we need Him.** When we don't pray, it implies that we think we can handle everything on our own. But the truth is that we cannot handle anything on our own. We need God for everything. We need Him to save us, forgive us, heal us, deliver us, fill us, restore us, redeem us, free us, guide us, protect us, lift us above our limitations, and move us into the plans and purposes He has for us. We can't get there without Him. When we pray, we're saying, "Lord, I can't live without you, and if you don't intervene in my life nothing good is going to happen."

**Prayer is making our request known to God.** It means sharing with Him all that is on our hearts, knowing that He cares about each one of those things. God promises to give us all we need, but in order to receive our needs, we must ask for it. Just as He instructs us to ask for our daily bread, we are to come before Him and ask for whatever else we need also.

**Prayer is not a last resort.** It is something we turn to when all else fails – a stab at something in the dark, or an exercise in positive thinking to try and make ourselves feel better. Prayer changes things, but we must talk to God about the things that need to be changed. Prayer is acknowledging that even though what we are praying for may seem impossible to us, but with God all things are possible (Matthews 19:26).

# *Type of Prayers*

There are various types of prayers. Because of the fact that the various types of prayers are connected and permits a flow from one type to another, it is difficult to conceive of them in term of rigid classifications. They are enumerated here more on the basis of psychology than on history. Here, I have listed several types of prayers:[5]

1.  **Thanksgiving:** Expresses gratitude to God. It is used in blessing your food, when given gifts, or offertory prayer. Thanksgiving honors God, and to praise Him with gratitude. It is developed out of meditation or experiences of religious elevation and utilized various patterns in both public and private ceremonies. It is a vital part of prayer.

2.  **Praise and Worship:** Is developed out of meditation or experiences of religious elevation and utilizes various patterns in both public and private ceremonies. Worship is reverence, admiration, and devotion expression to God. With praise and worship – you enters into God's presence. *Enter into His gates with thanksgiving, and into His courts with praise; be thankful unto Him and bless His name (Psalms 100:4).*

---

[5]  https://www.britannica.com/topic/prayer/Types-of-prayer

**Worship** is the giving of honor and devotion. **Praise** is thanksgiving an expression of gratitude not only for what God has done, but also for who He is. You are to worship God in spirit and in truth: *But the hour cometh, and now is when the true worshippers shall worship the Father in spirit and in truth. For the Father seeketh such to worship Him. God is a Spirit, and they that worship Him must worship Him in spirit and in truth.*

Worshipping God in Truth means that you worship Him on the basis of what is revealed in the Word of God. To worship Him in spirit is to do so sincerely in the power of the Holy Ghost, from your innermost being, putting Him first above all others. When you worship in spirit, you allow the Holy Spirit to direct your worship. You do not use man-made formulas or rituals of worship. You do not repeat chants or prayers while your mind is somewhere else. Instead, you open up the innermost recesses of your heart and mind, and lift praise and adoration to Him in your own words. Sometimes the Holly Spirit will take over completely, and you will begin to worship in other tongues of your prayer language.

3. **Petition Prayer:** This is where we tell God of our needs and the concerns of our hearts. An honest request may sometimes be a contestable prayer. It is impossible to refuse to recognize the importance of request, whether it is for a material or spiritual gift or accomplishment. The requests that occur most often are for preservation of or return to health, the healing of the sick, long life, material goods, prosperity, or success in one's undertakings. Request for such as gold, may be tied to a magical invocation. It may also be a deviation from prayer when it takes the

form of a bargain or of a request for payment due. In payment of our praise, give to the head of the family who is imploring you glory and riches. Christianity has never condemned material requests but, rather has integrated them into a single providential order while at the same time subordinating them to spiritual values. In essence though not always in practice, requests are only on the fringe of prayer. As a religion adopts more spiritual goals, the requests become more spiritual. Petition must be made according to the will of God, as revealed in His written word for this type of prayer.

4. **Praying in the Spirit:** This term is derived from Jude 20 and 1 Corinthians 14:15. In the first case (Jude 20), the Holy Ghost appears to be the one praying; but in Paul case, the meaning seems to be praying from his own spirit. Both may be defined as prayer that arises from the merging of the human spirit with the Holy Ghost in prayer. In some instances, such prayer is in other tongues, which enables the Holy Spirit to intercede according to God's Will, unaffected by the intellect or desires of the one praying.

5. **Mystical Union or Ecstasy:** Ecstasy is literally a departure from, a tearing away from, or a surpassing of human limitations and also a meeting with and embracing of the divine. It is a fusion of being with being, in which the mystic experiences a union that he characterizes as a nuptial union such as "God is in me and I am in him". [6]The mystic experiences God himself in an inexpressible encounter because it is beyond the ordinary experiences

---

[6] https://kids.britannica.com/students/article/prayer/109489/66256-toc

of man. The mystical union may be a lucid and conscious progression of contemplative prayer, or it may make a more passive form of a seizing by God of the one who is praying. Ecstatic prayer goes beyond the frame of ordinary prayer and becomes an experience in which words fail. Mystics speak in turn of unity, pleasure, or of intoxication. It is found in the accounts of Hindu, Persian, Hellenistic, and Christian mystics.

6.  **Adoration**: It's a demonstration of love, devotion, and respect for God. The way to adore God is to reflect on the attributes of His character, such as His goodness, mercy, long-suffering, etc. Adoration takes on the fullest meaning in the presence of the transcendental God who reveals Himself to man in the religions of revelation. In the Old Testament, Isaiah's vision of the holy one (Isaiah 6:3), the seraphim chant to God; Holy, Holy is the Lord of host; the whole earth is full of His glory. This hymn of adoration became a part of the Christian liturgy. The supreme form of adoration, however, is generally considered to be holy and silence, which can be found in primitive religion and in ancient religions, as well as in the higher religions, and among mystics. It expresses the most adequate attitude toward the immeasurable mystery of God.

7.  **Commitment:** This is the prayer of committing your life and will to God. It includes prayers of consecration and dedication to God, His work, and His purposes.

8.  **Confession and Repentance:** Acknowledging one's sin or affirming God's greatness and goodness. This is where we open our heart to God and ask him to reveal all sin in our lives so He can forgive us and cleanse us.

Confession expresses at the same time an affirmation of faith and recognition of the state of sin. In Mazdeism, as in ancient Christianity, the confession of faith accompanies the renunciation of demons. The confessions of Saint Augustine also illustrate this dual theme. In a similar fashion, ancient and primitive men recognize that their sins unlash the anger of the gods.

The admission of sin cannot be explained only by anguish or by the feeling of guilt; it is also related to what is deepest in man, to what constitutes his being and his action. Confession is viewed as the first step toward salvation in both Judaism and Christianity. In Buddhism, monks confess their sins publicly before the Buddha and the congregation twice a month. Situated at the most personal level of man, sin places him directly before God, who alone is able to grant pardon and salvation.

9. **Contrition:** Means grieving and being truly sorry for one's sin.

10. **Entreaty:** To plead and ask urgently in order to persuade. Exodus 8:8-9 is a prime example, where Pharaoh asked Moses to entreat God for the plague to depart. In other passages, the words beseech, exhort, ask and pray are used with the same meaning (James 3:17).

11. **Meditation:** To meditate is to focus thoughts on, reflect on, or ponder somethings. Meditation should be a part of prayer, as one quietly reflects on God's Word.

12. **Miserere:** which means, "Have Mercy" (Ps. 51:1)? Of the ancient Israelite, King David expresses repentance for sin with an intensity and dept. that has a universal value. One of the results of such a dialogue with God is the discovery of the dark depth of sin.

    In reference to Daniel 9:15-19, after Daniel had prayed his prayer of confession, he offers a petition prayer whereas he prayed, negatively, for God's wrath against his people to be satisfied, at ease, and positively, for God's grace, mercy, and forgiveness to be displayed in the people's restoration to their land.

13. **Intercession:** This is where we pray for others. Members of primitive societies have a clear sense of their solidarity in the framework of the family, the clans, and the tribes. This solidarity is often expressed in intercessory prayer, in which the needs of others are expressed. In such societies, the head of the family prays for the other members of the family, but his prayers also are extended to the whole tribe, especially to its chief; the primitive may pray even for those who are not members of his tribe.

    Intercessory prayers are also significant in Eastern and Ancient religions. In the hymns of the Rigveda the father implores the god for all of those who owe him their lives and are his family. In the Greek play, the mother, on her death, entrusts the orphans she is about to leave to Hestia, the goddess of the home. Among the Babylonians and the Assyrians, priesthood was established primarily to say prayers of intercession.

In biblical religion, intercession is spiritualized in view of a consciousness of the messianic mission. Moses views himself as one with his peoples even when they fail in their duty. Pardon your people, he prays, or remove me from the Book of Life. Such solidarity finds its supreme form in the prayer of Christ on the cross when He said, "Father, forgive them, for they know not what they do".[7]

There is power in intercession. The power of intercession is based on our relationship with God. It is entering into a partnership with God. Therefore, we need to get to know God's character, because if we know God's character, we know what God will do tomorrow.

The ministry of intercession for the world is the greatest ministry we can have. Jesus, in His greatest prayer in John 17:9, said, "I pray for them – I pray not for the world". Jesus' ministry in heaven is just that. He is praying for us.

We must accept our responsibility. We must pray for the world. We become intercessors as we pray for a lost city, as we pray for a lost nation, as we pray for a seemingly lost cause. As we do so, we do the will of God. If something that happens in the world which, without that prayer, would not have happened. That's the power of our intercession.

We have been called to share the throne life of God. We are not puppets in the hands of an Almighty God who just pulls the strings. We are people with whom He wants to deal with. We are people who can become intimate with a God we can know and understand. That relationship is

---

[7] https://www.britannica.com/topic/prayer/Types-of-prayer#ref66253

the secret. Nevertheless, you must open the door in your life to real intercession.

14. **Submission:** A submissive person humbly accepts the authority and lordship of God as he prays. The Bible also speaks of the attitude of submission to the leaders God places over you (Hebrews 13:7).

15. **Supplication:** Supplication means beseeching God or strongly appealing to Him in behalf of a need. This includes the idea of intercession, petition, and strong requests. In some passages they are translated as "begging for mercy or favor. It is a passionate pleading with God.

16. **Travail:** It is referred to as "a painful work or toil". Either physical or mental. It is frequently associated with childbirth. Paul compared his prayerful concern for the spiritual health of the Galatian believers to the pangs of childbirth (Galatians 4:19).

# *Power of Prayer*

Here, I've learned that there is very little power in the key that fits my car. The car engine has power, but it does not come to life without my key being put into the ignition. In other words I don't have the power to go outside and get myself going 75 miles an hour, but I have access to a resource that can get me moving at that speed.

Jesus said, "I will give you the keys of the kingdom of heaven". Keys mean the authority, the privilege, and the access. Some things will not be turned on unless you turn them on. Some things will not be turned loose unless you turn them loose. Some things will not be set free unless you set them free. The key doesn't make the power of the engine; it only releases the power of the engine.

Having legal possession of the keys to a car was evidence that we have the right to that car. In the same way, Jesus gives us the keys of His kingdom; we have the right to come before God in prayer. "As many as received Him to them He gave the right to become children of God". As His children we have the right to come before our Heavenly Father in prayer.

Having the keys to the car also means that we have the responsibility for it. In that same way, we are responsible for our side of the partnership with God in prayer. If we don't use the key of prayer, then it is likely that nothing will happen. In other words, there won't be anything released or unlocked.

Our problem is that we sometimes forget where we put the keys to our car. The same is true in our prayer life. We have a tendency to misplace the key that unlocks God's power. We come upon a situation or a situation comes upon us, and we forget to use our key of prayer to move powerfully in and through it. Whenever I lose the keys to my car, I ask God to show me where they are and help me to find them and He does. He always does. Whenever we lose sight of our prayer key, we can ask Him to help us find it again.

Now, a key is no good to us if we never use it to unlock anything. If a car key doesn't connect with the ignition, the power of the engine will not function. God's power is always available to us, but if we don't use the key of prayer, we can't appropriate this power for our lives.

There are many good people out there who love God, reads His Word, and prays, but they can't see His power moving in response to their prayers. Their lives don't seem to affect or change the world around them for God's kingdom; therefore the world looks upon their faith as being irrelevant. Often the reason for that is many people don't understand the need to ask for the Holy Ghost power.

People sometime hesitate to pray because they do not understand the power of the Holy Ghost working through them when they do or either they don't believe God's power is there for them. But God let us know that prayer is available to all who love Him with their whole being and love others as themselves.

I don't mean we don't benefit from God's power – we most certainly do - every day. Whenever we acknowledge that we need a fresh flow of God's power working in us and ask for His Holy Spirit to flow through us as we pray, we will see His power move in our lives. But, He wants us to recognize that His Spirit is love. His love must be the motivating force behind everything we do and each pray we pray. In order to do this we must first submit ourselves to God and wait at His feet in prayer. It is not that He is trying to keep His power from us. It is that He wants us to depend on Him for it.

God's power is made available to us in order to do two things. One is to accomplish God's purposes here on earth. The other is to give evidence to people around us that Jesus is still alive. We cannot do either of those things if we pray without being clothed with the power from heaven. Without the power of the Holy Ghost, we are praying uncovered.

Once you experience the power of God in your life through prayer, you will never be the same – nor will you settle for anything less. Jesus always moved by the influence of the Holy Ghost. His disciples observed that. They personally witnessed Him healing people, casting out demons, and performing many other miracles, and they wanted to know how these things happened. They recognized that Jesus had a source of power they didn't have. They also saw Him frequently go to a private place and pray, and whenever he did, the life and power of God would be infused in Him. They obviously knew there was a connection between power and prayer because they didn't ask Him to teach them how to get power. They asked Him to teach them how to pray. And what He taught them is now known as the Lord's Prayer (Matthew 6:9-13).

In everything Jesus did on earth, He did not depend on His own resources and power as God. Although He was God, He chose to walk as a human being. When the Son of God became flesh, He laid aside His divine prerogatives as God and became entirely dependent upon the resources of the Holy Ghost. He did all this voluntarily – never becoming less than God, but in humility chose to walk among us as a human being.

Even though Jesus was the Son of God, He didn't hesitate going to His father in prayer in order to receive power for all He needed to do. He teaches us how to do the same. God wants us to draw on His resources by coming to Him in prayer and seeking a fresh infusion of power the way Jesus did.

Jesus did not teach His disciples the Lord's Prayer so they would have something to recite over and over. He was teaching them how to release the power they needed. He said the way to pray is to first of all, recognize that God is your Father. (Our Father which are in heaven) That's the ground for the relationship. Second, worship Him. (Hallowed be thou name). His great name – we are directed to pray with boldness. (Thou kingdom come, thou will be done on earth as it is in heaven). These words invoke at earth level what God has ordained at heaven's level.

Many people think praying "Thou kingdom come is a prayer about something in the future, but it's not a someday prayer. Just like give us this day our daily bread, and forgive us our debt is not talking about someday in the future. It is referring to now. Therefore when we pray "Thou kingdom come, we are asking God's kingdom to invade our circumstances right now.

Now, just like Jesus, we need to be empowered by the Holy Ghost in all we say and do. He is our teacher, helper, and guider, and we must ask Him to teach us how to pray with fervent and passion so that our prayers have power. We must request that He help us to have love and compassion for others, even those who are hard to love, so that our prayers are rightly motivated. We must invite Him to be in the driver's seat of our lives so that He can guide us where we need to go. When we move through each Paul spent several days with the disciples under His influence we will accomplish things we would otherwise never be able to do.

**There are three roads that a person can choose to travel in life**: (1) the way of Satan.

(2) The way of self and (3) the way of God. We have a choice as to which road we want to travel. It is highly dangerous to make the wrong choice.

Now if you should go (Satan) the devils' way – it leads to darkness, destruction, and death because he is a thief who comes to steal, kill, and to destroy. If you decide to choose your own way, nothing will turn out as good as it could have in our lives, plus, we will eventually end up going Satan's way because he is the originator of having it your own way. Nevertheless, if you go God's way, you will end up in a realm that brings life and hope, because it gives you power over self and Satan.

One of the dangers we must look out for when traveling through life is forgetting who we are and where we are going.

The day we were born again, we received new citizenship papers. Our name was written in the Lamb's Book of Life. We were registered in Heaven. We are now traveling with papers proving that we were born into God's kingdom and we represent a higher authority and power than any force hell.

God wants to use us for His kingdom purposes. And that is what we want as well. We don't want to just read about God, we want His life in us. We want His anointing upon us in such a way that when people see us or talk to us, they see that Jesus is alive. We want people to be attracted to Jesus because of what they see of Him in us.

When God brought the Israelites out of Egypt, He told them that if they would walk in His ways that He would make them a kingdom of priests, and they would be a people who moved in a realm of authority that was related to the priesthood. They would have a relationship with the one who was the head of the kingdom. Nevertheless, Israel lost that opportunity because they did not want what God had in store for them; and as a result, they never arrived where God intended for them to go. We must arrive where God intends for us to go, because we wants what God wants (1 Peter 2:5-9).

God wants to pour out His Spirit upon each of us, and enables us to become ambassadors of His kingdom. He wants to take people who are willing to surrender their lives to Him and show them how to live by the power of His Spirit. We want that as well, because we know we will never be able to pray effectively unless we move in the power that give evidence of God's presence in our lives. The world around us is too frightening, dangerous, and unpredictable to not be certain that we have access to a power that can make a major difference when we pray.

Now let us take another look at **The Power of Prayer.** In Revelation, Chapter 5, we are given an illustration of the great power that God has placed in the hands of His people through prayer. John was given a glimpse of God seated upon His throne. Around the throne were twenty four (24) elders, and four (4) angelic beings, all worshipping God.

The Lion of the tribe of Judah, who appeared as the Lamb of God who had been slain, came about and took the scroll from the right hand of God.

Think about the excitement and glory at that moment, as Christ, the Lamb of God, the Redeemer, the Mighty Conqueror, the Lion of the tribe of Judah, steps forward and takes the scroll from the right hand of God: The four cherubim, the twenty and four elders, and the thousands upon thousands of angels surrounding the throne are all watching in holy reverence and awe. God great end-time plan is about to be revealed.

Before Christ breaks the seals unfolding the events in His end-time plan, the prayers and praises symbolized by the harps of the saints are offered up to God. All of heaven resounds with a mighty roar of praises as all of creation joins this heavenly host in worshipping God and the Lamb. Our prayers here on earth on behalf of the lost, our cries to Him regarding the wickedness and immorality surrounding us and for Gods will and purposes to be fulfilled, do not disappear into thin air. They are not forgotten. They ascend before God and are as sweet smelling incense in His nostrils.

The same way Aaron, on the Day of Atonement, took the censer full of burning coals off and went into the holy of holies and offered up incense before the Mercy Seat, the angel will take the censer with the incense and prayers and impregnate the air with this holy offering.

Also, the worship in the Old Testament tabernacle was to be a type of this heavenly worship. The Mercy Seat was where God appeared in a glory cloud. God directed that Aaron, the high priest, covered the Mercy Seat with a cloud of incense. The cloud of incense covering the Mercy Seat in the tabernacle was symbolic of the cloud of incense mixed with the prayers of God's people that will be offered to God upon His throne before His judgments are poured out upon the earth. This heavenly scenario reveals the tremendous significance and value that God places upon our prayers.

# *The Audience of Prayer*

No religion has ever had a higher standard and priority for prayer than Judaism. As God's chosen people the Jews were the recipients of His written Word, "entrusted with the oracles of God". God spoke directly to Him. No other person, as a race or as a nation, has ever been so favored by God or had such direct communication with Him. Of all people, they should have known how to pray. But they did not like every other aspect of their religious life; their praying had been corrupted and perverted by rabbinical tradition. Most Jews were completely confused about how to pray, as God wanted.

Over the years a number of faults had crept into Jewish prayer life. For one thing, prayer had become ritualized. The wording and forms of prayer were set, and were then simply read or repeated from memory. Such prayers could be given with almost no attention being paid to what was said. They were a routine, semiconscious religious exercise.

**First fault,** the ritual prayers could be given with three basic attitudes: sincerity, indifference, or pride. Those Jews whose hearts were right, used the times of prayer to worship and glorify God. They thought about the words and sincerely believed what they prayed: Others went through the words perfunctorily, mumbling the syllables as fast as possible in order to finish. Others, such as the scribes and Pharisees, recited the prayers meticulously, making sure to enunciate every word and syllable properly. Three times a day they had a ready-made opportunity to parade their pious.

**A second fault,** had crept into the Jewish prayer life was the development of prescribed prayers for every object and every occasion. There were prayers for light, darkness, fire, rain, the new moon, traveling, good news, bad news, and so on. No doubt the original intent was to bring every aspect of life into the presence of God; but by making the prayers prescribed and formalized that purpose was undermined.

**A third fault** which was mention earlier was the practice of limiting prayer to specific times and occasions. Prayer was offered when the given time came or situation arose, with no relation to genuine desire or need. As with prescribed wording, prescribed times did not prevent true prayer from being offered. Many faithful Jews like Daniel (Daniel 6:10) used times as reminders to open their hearts to the Lord. Even in the early church, because most Christians were Jews and still worshipped at the Temple and in the synagogues, the traditional hours of prayer were often observed (Acts 3:1, 10:3-30).

**A Fourth fault** was in esteeming long prayers, believing that a prayer's sanctity and effectiveness were in direct proportion to its length. Jesus warned of the scribes who, "for appearance's sake offered long prayers" (Mark 12:40). A long prayer, of course, is not necessarily an insincere prayer, but, a long public prayer lends itself to pretense, repetition, and many other such dangers. The fault is in praying for appearance's sake to impress others with our religiosity.

The ancient rabbis felt that the longer the prayer, the more likely it would be heard and heeded by God. Verbosity was confused with meaning, and length was confused with sincerity.

**A fifth fault** that had been singled out by Jesus in Matthew 6:7 were that of meaningless repetitions, patterned after those of pagan religions. In their contest with Elijah on Mount Carmel, the pagan prophets called on the name of God from morning until noon saying, "O Baal, answer us", and they raved until the time of the offering of the evening sacrifice (1 Kings 18: 26-29). Hour after hour they repeated the same phrase, trying by the very quantity of their words to make their god hear and respond.

Throughout the centuries the Jews had been influenced by practices from the pagan. They often added adjective after adjective before God's name in their prayers, apparently trying to out-do one another in mentioning His divine attributes.

**The worst fault,** however, was that of wanting to be seen and heard by other people, especially their fellow Jews. Most of the other faults were not necessarily wrong in them, but were carried to extremes and used in meaningless ways. But, this fault was intrinsically evil, because it both came from and was intended to satisfy pride. Whatever form the prayer may have taken, the motive was sinful self-glory, the ultimate perversion of this sacred means of glorifying God (John 14:13).

**Despicable fault,** this is the fault that Jesus zeroes in on. And when you pray, you are not to be as the hypocrites. Prayer that focuses on self is always hypocritical, because by definition, the focus of every prayer should be on God. As mentioned in the last chapter, the term hypocrite originally referred to actors who used large masks to portray the roles they were playing. Hypocrites are actors, pretenders, and persons who play a role. What they say and do does not represent what they themselves feel or believe but only the image they hope to create.

The hypocritical Scribes and Pharisees prayed for the same purpose. They did everything possible to attract attention and bring honor to themselves. This was the essence of their righteousness, which Jesus said had no part in His Kingdom (See Matthews 5:20).

One of the greatest dangers to religion is that folks simply allow self to become their religious belief. The hypocrites, who Jesus spoke of, had convinced themselves that by performing certain religious acts, including various types of prayer, that it would be acceptable to God. People today still deceive themselves into thinking they are Christians, when all they have done is dress their old nature in religious trappings.

Nothing is so sacred the Satan will not invade it. In fact, the more sacred something is, the more he desires to profane it. Naturally, a few things please him more than to come between believers and their Lord in the sacred intimacy of prayer. Sin will follow us into the very presence of God: and no sin is more powerful or destructive than pride. In those moments when we would come before the Lord in worship and purity of heart, we may be tempted to worship ourselves.

I have learned in the scriptural that Jesus two most intense times of spiritual opposition were during His forty days of solitude in the wilderness and during His prayer in the Garden of Gethsemane on the night He was betrayed and arrested. On both occasions He was alone praying to His Father. It was in the most private and holy place of communion that Satan presented his strongest temptations before the Son of God. The hypocrites loved to stand and pray. Standing was a normal position for prayer among the Jews.

In the Old Testament we see God's faithful praying while kneeling, and standing. In the New Testament times standing was the most common position, and did not necessarily indicate a desire to be. The synagogues were the most appropriate and likely places for public prayers to be offered. It was the place where Jews worshipped most often, especially those who lived great distances from the Temple. The synagogue was the local place of assembly, not only for worship but also for various civic and social gatherings. If done sincerely, prayer at any of those functions was appropriate. The street corners were also a normal place for prayer, because devout Jews would stop wherever they were at the appointed hour for prayer, even if they were walking down the street or visiting at the corner. But, the word used here for street is not the same as that in Matthew 6:2, which refer to a narrow street. The word used here refers to a wide major street, or a major street corner, where a crowd was most likely to be.

**The Implied fault:** Here is where the hypocrites loved to pray where they would have a large audience. There was nothing wrong with praying at a major intersection if that was where you happened to be at the time for prayer. But something was very much wrong if you planned to be there at prayer time for the specific purpose of praying where the most people could see you.

The real evil of those hypocritical worshipers, rather in the synagogues or on the street therefore corners, was the desire to display them in order to be seen of men. It was not wrong to pray in those places, but they happened to afford the largest audiences, and were the places where the hypocrites preferred to pray.

Now, as always, sin began in the heart. It was pride, the desire to exalt themselves before their fellow Jews that was the root of the sin. Like the Pharisees in Jesus' parable – those hypocrites ended up praying to themselves and before other people. God had no part (See Luke 18:11). Some overly reactionary believers have used these warnings of Jesus as a reason to renounce all public prayer. But, the Lord taught no such thing. He Himself often prayed in the presence of His disciples (Lk. 11:1), and in public, as when He blessed food before feeding the multitudes (Matthew 14:19).

The scripture records many public prayers that were entirely appropriate and sincere. At the dedication of the Temple, Solomon prayed an extended, detailed prayer before all the Priests, Levites, and leaders of Israel (second Chronicles 6:12-42).

When they were under Ezra's leadership, the covenant was renewed after the Exile; a group of eight Levites offered a heartfelt, moving prayer of repentance before all the people (Nehemiah 9:5-38). After Peter and John were arrested, questioned, and then released by the Sanhedrin shortly after Pentecost, the whole group of their companions rejoiced and lifted their voices to God with one accord (Acts 4:24).

But, the public prayers of the typical Scribe or Pharisees were ritualistic, mechanical, inordinately long, repetitious, and above all ostentatious like the hypocrites who gave for the sake of men's praise (Matt. 6:2) – those who prayed for the sake of men's praise also had their reward in full. They were concerned only about the reward men could give, and that is all the reward they received.

# *The True Audience of God*

Now, let's take a look at the True Audience of God concerning prayer. The Bible tell us that when you pray, go into your inner room, and when you have shut your door, pray to your Father who are in secret, and your Father who sees in secret will repay you (Matthew 6:6).

The basic definition of prayer as I mention earlier is "communion with God", and if He is not involved, then, it's only the pretense of prayer. Not only must He be involved, but centrally involved. Prayer is God's idea, not men. There could be no prayer if God did not condescend to speak with us, and we could not know how to pray had He not chosen to instruct us.

Jesus' teaching here is simple, in contrast to the complicated and difficult traditions. The phrase when you pray implies great latitude. The Lord gives no prescribed time or occasion. The inner room could be any sort of small room, chamber, or even a storage closet. Such rooms were often secret and used to store valued possessions for protection. The idea is that of going to the most private place available.

As I have previously said, Jesus does not forbid or condemn public prayer as such (First Timothy 2:1-4). Where Paul exhorted to pray and give thanks to all men. Paul said, "I exhort therefore, that first of all, supplications, prayers, intercessions, and giving of thanks be made for all men"; for Kings, and for all that are in authority; that we may lead a quiet and peaceable life in all godliness and honesty. For this is good and acceptable in the sight of God our Savior. First and most important of all, prayer is to hold the preeminent place in church meetings.

There are four types of prayers mentioned here: (1) **Supplications** are precise requests for specific needs, (2) **Prayers**, a general word embracing various kind of prayers such as: confession, adoration, and so on; (3) **Intercessions**: denote prayers to God on behalf of others, and (4) **Thanksgiving**, that refers to prayers of praise. Moreover, there are three reasons why the prayers in verse one is to be offered for all men. 1. That Christians may enjoy a tranquil life. 2. Such praying is good and acceptable to God. 3. It helps to bring about the salvation of men in verse four. In verse two, it mentions a quiet and peaceable life in all goodliness and honesty.

Now the word quiet means, "not troubled from without", that is, intercessory prayer that enables good government to ensure that enemies or forces outside its borders do not trouble its citizens. Peaceable means "not troubled from within"; that is the church's prayer also helps competent government, in maintaining law and order within its own borders. The translation godliness and honesty is unfortunate, for the exercise of these virtues is not dependent upon good government; they can be cultivated even in poor political management and persecution. Respect can be realized when rulers are competent and rightly discharging their duties. Otherwise, it is difficult to respect rulers when they are incompetent and unjust.

Jesus' purpose here seems to have been to make the greatest contrast possible to the practices of the Scribes, Pharisees, and other hypocritical religionists. The primary point Jesus makes does not have to do with location but with attitude. If necessary, Jesus says go to the most secluded private place you can find so you will not be tempted to show off. Go there and shut the door. Shut out everything else so that you can concentrate on God and pray to your Father. Do whatever you have to do to get your attention away from yourself and others and on Him and Him alone.

Much of our prayers life should be literally in secret. Jesus regularly went away from His disciples to pray entirely alone. Our family members or friends may know that we are praying, but what we say is not meant for them to hear. Back in the days, many Christians prayed so loud in their rooms that everyone down the hall heard what they said. If people sometimes happen to overhear our private prayers, it should not be b our intentions.

Therefore, the Father being in secret does not mean He is not present when we pray in public or with our families or other small groups of believers. He is very much present whenever His children call on Him. Jesus point has to do with the singleness of intention. True prayer is always intimate. Even prayer in public, if the heart is right and concentrated on God, will in a real and profound way shut one up alone in the presence of God.

In the pattern of prayer Jesus taught His disciples; He begins with Our Father (Matthew 6:9), indicating that other believers may be present and that the prayer is corporate. But even when prayer represents the feeling and needs of others who are present, the supreme attention is to be on God. In that sense, even the most public prayer is in secret. Even if the whole world hears what we say, there is an intimacy and focus on God in that communion that is unaffected.

God also sees in secret in the sense that He never betrays a confidence. Many things we share with God in our private prayers are for Him alone to know. Confidences we share even with our dearest loved ones or closest friends may sometimes be betrayed. Moreover, we can be sure that our secrets with God will forever be just that, and that one believer praying in secret with a pure heart has the full attention of the Father.

Furthermore, when our prayer is as it should be, our Father who sees in secret will repay us. The most important secret He sees is not the words we say in the privacy of our room, but the thoughts we have in the privacy of our heart. Those are the secrets about which He is supremely concerned, and about which only He can know with certainty (1 Corinthians 4:3-5). Those secrets sometimes are hidden even from us, because it is so easy to be deceived about our own motives.

When God is the audience of our prayer, we will have the reward only He can give. Jesus gives no idea in this passage as to what God's reward or repayment will be. The important truth is that God will faithfully and unfailingly bless those who come to Him in sincerity. Without question, the Lord will repay. Those who pray insincerely and hypocritically will receive the world's reward, and those who pray sincerely and humbly will receive God's reward.

God is not asking us to take a theology course before we come to Him. He simply wants us to share honestly from our heart. The right way to pray comes out of a heart that loves God and desires to communicate with Him.

# *Pray without Hypocrisy*

When you pray, you are not to be as the hypocrites: for they love to stand and pray in the synagogues and on the street corners, in order to be seen by men. But when you pray, go into your inner room, and when you have shut your door, pray to your Father who is in secret, and your Father who sees in secret will repay you. When you are praying, do not use meaningless repetition, as the Heathens do – for they suppose that they will be heard for their many words. Therefore do not be like them; for you Father knows what you need, before you ask Him.

None of us can comprehend exactly how prayer functions within the infinite mind and plan of God. The Calvinistic view emphasizes God's sovereignty, and in its extreme application holds that God will work according to His perfect will. At the opposite extreme, the Armenian view holds that God's actions pertaining to us are determined largely on the basis of our prayers. On the other hand, prayer is seen simply as a way of lining up with God regarding what He has already determined to do, and on the other hand it is beseeching God to do what He otherwise would not do.

The scripture supports both of those views and holds them, as it were, in tension. The Bible is unequivocal about God's absolute sovereignty: But it is equally unequivocal in declaring that within His sovereignty God calls on His people to beseech Him in prayer to implore His help in guidance, provision, protection, mercy, forgiveness, and countless other needs.

It is not required, nor possible to fathom the divine working that makes prayer effective. God simply commands us to obey the principles of prayer that His word gives. Our Lord's teaching in the present passage contains some of those principles.

Jesus continues His contrast of true and false righteousness, in particular the false righteousness typified by the Scribes and Pharisees exposes their hypocritical giving and their hypocritical lasting, expose their equally hypocritical praying. The prayers were defective in their intended audience and in their content.

# *Unsolved Prayer*

You've probably heard about the power of prayer and how prayer can bring about wonderful changes in your life. But have you ever prayed and nothing happened? Have you ever recited the same words over and over, hoping God would somehow help you make a decision or supply an answer to an unsolved problem? It's not that God doesn't care. The problem could be that you don't know what Jesus taught about prayer.

Have you ever stood in a church service and like some mechanical drone recited these words: "Our Father which art in heaven, hallowed be thy name, Thy kingdom come, Thy will be done in earth, as it is in heaven, give us this day our daily bread, and forgive us our debts, as we forgive our debtors, and lead us not into temptation, but deliver us from evil: For thine is the kingdom, and the power, and the glory, forever, Amen. Then, you walked away with no understanding of the kingdom, no power and no glory of God in your life. Does this sound familiar to you?

This passage is commonly called the Lord's Prayer, found in Matthews 6:9-13. Yet what Jesus gave here is actually an outline of how to approach God and is more accurately a model prayer. Let's consider what it reveals.

Let's start with proper focus and priorities. Taking a careful look at the model prayer, we see that Jesus says to begin your prayer by honoring God. How many times have you started your talk with God with the "gimmes"? Like give me a new car; give me a new job, or give me a new house or etc.

Jesus want us to begin our pray with praises for God's greatness. Many times we approach the awesome God as if He were a genius in a bottle waiting to grant us our wishes, instead of with an attitude of humble worship that is due the Creator of the universe. He then said to pray, Thy kingdom come. We must long for God's rule to be established throughout this earth and in our own lives today.

Now, what are the important priorities in your life? In the Sermon on the Mount, Jesus told His followers not to have anxious worry about their physical appearance or clothing. He told them to look at God's creation and see the power, love and genius of the Creator and trust in Him.

In Matthews 6:33, Jesus told His disciples not to fret over daily needs, but to seek first the kingdom of God and His righteousness, and all these things shall be added to you. God blesses those who have set His priorities in their lives. If you don't see God's blessings in your life, you should ask yourself, "Is God's priorities the main priorities in my life?"

Now, if you're going to have God fulfill His purpose in your life, then everything you do must be founded on two simple principles. Jesus said that the two greatest commandments are to love the Lord your God with all your heart, soul, and mind, and to love your neighbor as yourself (Matt. 22:37 - 40). These two commandments must be the basis of all your priorities if you want to receive God's blessings.

In this model prayer we are told to pray, "Your will be done on earth, as it is in heaven". In your relationship with the Creator, He grants you no terms except unconditional surrender. Unconditional surrender means to give up control over your own life and give your life to God. Handing over control of your life to God is daunting.

To accept God's willed in your life, you must have faith in His promised outcome for you. When you have that kind of trust in God, His power is unleashed in your life. It's not always easy, but God will be with you through all the ups and downs, and He will ensure the final victory.

Next, Jesus said to pray, "Give us this day our daily bread". Now, it is important that we take our physical needs to God. But notice, you do this after you have honored Him and asked for His will in your life. God wants you to bring your job needs, bodily aches and pains, family problems and financial difficulties to Him for wisdom and counsel. He wants to intervene in your life to make every day a wonderful, spiritual adventure, but first you must acknowledge Him as the source of your life and blessings. If you put God and His way first, He will see to it that all our needs are met.

In this next outline we will talk about forgive to be forgiven which Christ gave when He said, "Forgive us our debts, as we forgive our debtors". The debt here is what we owe for the sin we have committed. Thankfully, God offers us forgiveness for the terrible things we've done against Him. In return, He expects all of us to extend forgiveness to others.

Forgiveness is giving up the emotional need to punish someone who has treated us in a hurtful way. A disciple of Jesus named Peter realized that to forgive someone seven times was remarkable. Jesus told him to forgive a great deal more than that (See Matthew 18:21-22). Forgiving others isn't easy, but you will never experience true peace of mind until you do.

Jesus explained the need for forgiving others in a parable about a man who owed a king a great amount of money. The man was brought before the king and begged for time to get the money together. The king, out of the goodness of his heart, showed the man mercy and forgave him of his debt.

This man then went out and found another man who owed him a small debt. The second man begged for time, but the forgiven man demanded payment and threw the second man into debtor's prison. The king found out and told the man whom he'd forgiven, "Should you not also have had compassion on your fellow servant, just as I had pity on you? He then turned the man over to suffering until he paid what had previously been forgiven him. Here, Jesus warned, "So my Heavenly Father also will do to you if each of you, from his heart, does not forgive his brother his trespasses" (Matt. 8:23-35).

When you refuse to give up the desire for revenge, you not only twist your own emotions into anger and bitterness, you damage your ability to respond to God's forgiveness. Once you become obsessed with the wrong someone else has done, you start down a long road of anger and despair. You must replace the thoughts of hurtful treatment from others with positive thoughts of God in your life.

Next, in this model prayer, it says, "Lead us not into temptation, but deliver us from evil. Now the wording in the first part of this verse can be misleading, since God tempts no one (James 1:13). Instead, each one is tempted when he is drawn away by his own desires and enticed (verse 14).

The intent of Christ words is twofold: first, that we should understand we have an unseen spiritual enemy, Satan the devil (1 Peter 5:8), from whom we need to ask God for His protection and help; and second, that we might be humble and teachable enough to learn our lessons now so we won't have to be put through sore trials to be corrected.

We must be aware that Satan will use our weaknesses against us. Satan wants to enslave us to sin, but God wants to break whatever bond ties us down. Take your weakness to God and ask Him to protect you from situations that will tempt you to sin and from the tricks and temptations of the devil.

Jesus ends His prayer outline with an expression of confidence in God's ability to answer the prayer for: "Yours is the kingdom and the power and the glory forever, Amen". Once again, your prayer must end by praising God.

This model prayer isn't a magic formula where you recite the special words and power is released in your life. It is an outline teaching you how to have a personal relationship with your Creator. When you have trouble praying, use this outline to personalize your talk with your Creator. Learn to pray as Jesus prayed.

Sometimes I think the devil knows much more about the power of prayer than we as Christians do. I also know that we can unlock that secret power in our own lives if we learn how to focus our prayer as Jesus did.

Whenever Jesus prayed, things happened. No wonder the disciples asked Him to share the secret with them saying, "Lord teach us to pray". They said, even though they had been praying throughout their lives, in the synagogues and in their homes.

Prayer was the heart of His success, and it is also the key to our success as Christians. Yet too often we fail just where Jesus succeeded. The world has not yet seen what God can do through a person who is fully dedicated to Jesus Christ and understands the power of prayer.

Prayer is the basis of everything God is accomplishing in the world, and that is why I consider it so important for us to unlock these hidden reserves of divine power and confront the enemy who is sweeping the earth today.

Why don't you join me in attacking Satan's strongholds? You can provide prayer support for our fellow Christians – behind the enemies' line, in countries that deny religious freedom. Elijah was a man just like us. He prayed earnestly that it would not rain, and it did not rain on the land for three and a half years. Again he prayed, the heavens gave rain, and the earth produced its crops (James 5:17, 18 NIV).

# *The Model Prayer*

Now there are two versions of what is called "The Lord's Prayer or the Disciples Prayer", which actually should be called "The Model Prayer". One is recorded in Matthews 6: 9-13 and one is Luke 11: 2-4). Most Bible scholars agree that the similarities between them justify regarding the two versions as forms of the same prayer rather than different prayers. The disciples had watched Jesus pray and witnessed the power that resulted from His prayer experiences. This created in them a yearning desire to learn to pray as He did, so one of the disciples asked – "Lord teach us to pray" (Luke 11:1).

Jesus responded by *saying: After this manner therefore pray ye: Our Father which art in heaven, Hallowed be thy name. Thy kingdom come; Thy will be done in earth, as it is in heaven. Give us this day our daily bread. And forgive us our debts, as we forgive our debtors. And lead us not into temptation, but deliver us from evil: For thine is the kingdom, and the power, and the glory, forever Amen (Matthews 6:9-13).*

When the disciples came to Jesus, they said, Lord, teach us to pray – not teach us a prayer. They wanted to learn to pray like Jesus. The Lord responded by using a method commonly employed by Jewish Rabbis, who listed topics of truth, then under each point provided a complete outline.

Moreover, in this Model Prayer, Jesus used the same teaching pattern. He gave a general outline and said, "After this manner, therefore, pray ye, which in the Greek means to pray along these lines. Jesus did not teach His followers to repeat the prayer word-for-word, but rather to pray after this manner. It is a framework, not a formula, and within this divine framework, the Holy Spirit anoints us to pray.

This is a prayer for all true believers, as it begins with the plural possessive pronominal adjective "Our." Further in the prayer are statements like give us, lead us, and forgive us." In every sense, the model prayer is an intercessory prayer because you pray for others as well as yourself.

**Our Father which art in heaven:** Through the ages, Old Testament saints directed their prayers to the true and living God, the all-powerful Jehovah, and the Holy One of Israel. They knew Him as the Almighty God who rolled back the Red Sea, led them through the wilderness, rained down manna from heaven, caused water to gush forth from the rock, delivered them out of the fiery furnace, shut the mouths of lions, and delivered them out of the hands of their enemies. But they did not have an intimate relationship with Him as their Heavenly Father. No one in the Old Testament ever prayed to God as their Father.

The words "Our Father" indicate nearness, but the word "in heaven" implies distance. Psalm 139 reveals, however, that God is everywhere? When we pray to our Father in heaven, it does not emphasize the distance between the Father and us, but it brings us from the natural world to a powerful spiritual plane. It assures us that God has at His disposal the entire resources of the supernatural ream with which to respond to the requests presented in the remainder of the model prayer. When we pray "Our Father which art in heaven" we are immediately linked through Christ to a supernatural God with unlimited supernatural resources for intercessory prayer.

We address God as Father because we are His sons and daughters. *And because ye are sons, God hath sent forth the Spirit of his Son into you hearts, crying, Abba, Father. Wherefore thou art no more a servant, but a son; and if a son, then an heir of God through Christ (Galatians 4:6-7).*

In Matthew 7:7-11, Jesus emphasizes the fact that when we come to God in prayer, we are to come as a trusting child, asking in confidence, knowing that our Father will give us whatever we ask. Jesus said; *if ye then, being evil, know how to give good gifts unto your children, how much more shall your Father which is in heaven, give good things to them that ask him?*

**Hallowed be thy name:** When we become members of God's family, our heavenly Father's name is given to us, just as a child who is adopted in the natural world assumes the name of his new dad. Our spiritual adoption gives us the right to call God, our father, and receive all of the benefits associated with His name because we are now heirs of His kingdom. When we say, Hallowed be thy name, we proclaim the person, power, and authority of God.

**Thy Kingdom come:** In the Greek, Hebrew, and Aramaic language, the Kingdom of God refers to the kingship, sovereignty, reign, or ruling activity of God. It is the expression of God's nature in action. God's realm of operation can be viewed in terms of its inclusive universal organization as the kingdom of God; its local visible organization as the Church through which the Kingdom is extended; and individuals of which the kingdom is composed – that is - all true believer born into this kingdom.

Sometime in the future, the Kingdom of God will be established in visible form. We do not know the exact timing of this (Acts 1:7), but according to God's Word, it is certain that all of the kingdoms of the world will become the property of God. The evil kingdom of Satan will be defeated, and our King will reign forever (Revelation 11:15)

The centrality of the Kingdom message is clear in the New Testament. It is mentioned 49 times in the Book of Mark, and 38 times in the Book of Luke. Jesus began His earthly ministry by declaring the arrival of the kingdom (Matt. 4:17). He ended His earthly ministry by speaking of things pertaining to the Kingdom (Acts 1:3). In between the beginning and the end of His ministry, the emphasis was always on the Kingdom. He was constantly declaring that He must preach its message in other places (Luke 4:43). Every parable of Jesus related to the Kingdom, and His life patterned its principles.

Jesus taught that we, as believers, were to give similar emphasis to the kingdom: *But seek ye first the kingdom of God, and His righteousness; and all these things shall be added unto you (Matt. 6:33).* This verse indicates where we should focus our praying, preaching, teaching, and living. It should all be targeted on the Kingdom of God. If we seek first the Kingdom, it assures the answer to other petitions that follow in The Model Prayer.

Praying, thy kingdom come is more than a prayer for the return of Jesus and establishment of the Kingdom in its final form. We are actually declaring that our Father will reign in the lives of believers, unbelievers, and the entire earth. We are praying that life here on earth may be regulated by His commands, therefore, we are asking God to remove anything within ourselves and others that is in rebellion against His Kingdom – including words, attitudes, desires, behavior and etc.

**Thy will be done on earth as it is in heaven:** Now, in the Greek language there are two words used for the word "will" in reference to God. One word is **"Boulema"** referring to God's sovereign "will", which is His predetermined plan for everything that happens in the universe? This type of God's "will" is fulfilled, regardless of decisions made by man. God is at work to bring to pass all things on the basis of His sovereign "will": *In whom also we have obtained an inheritance, being predestinated according to the purpose of him who worketh all things after to the counsel of his own will (Ephesians 1:11).*

The **Boulema Will of God** does not require the cooperation of man because it outcome is predetermined since it is the written Word of God.

The other word for God's will is **"Thelema",** which refers to His individual will for each man and woman. People have the power to choose whether or not they will walk in the thelema Will of God. When you pray thy will be done over yourself and others, you are interceding for the thelema Will of God to be done.

**Give us this day our daily bread:** In the Model Prayer, we seek first the Kingdom when we declare thy kingdom come over every circumstance in our life. We submit to our Heavenly Father's will, declaring, Thy will be done. We can pray with assurance – give us this day our daily bread, asking that our needs be met to enable us to fulfill His will and extend His Kingdom.

Praying acknowledges us that God is our source, not a denomination, an inheritance, or a company paycheck. The Greek word translated to English as daily in the Model Prayer means "necessary or essential bread, sufficient for our sustenance and support". It's used in this context confirms that the Model Prayer Jesus taught is to be used daily as a framework for our prayers. The prayer is for both spiritual and material sustenance, and the word *"us"* denote that we are to intercede for provision for others as well as ourselves.

**And forgive us our debts, as we forgive our debtors:** Here, we must learn to both receive and give forgiveness for our own offenses and for the injustices caused by others. Personal offenses occur when you offend God through your own sin. You deal with these by asking Him to forgive you when you say, *forgive us our debts.* The Bible says: *"If we say that we have no sin, we deceive ourselves, and the truth is not in us. If we confess our sins, he is faithful and just to forgive us our sins, and to cleanse us from all unrighteousness (1 John 1:8-9).* When you confess your known sin, God forgives your unknown sin as well, and cleanse you from all unrighteousness.

The second area in which forgiveness must be manifested in is forgiving others. Jesus taught us to pray; forgive us our debts, as we forgive our debtors. The literal rendering of this verse in

Greek is "as we forgave our debtors". Nevertheless, the verse could read: Forgive us our debts, as we have forgiven others. The idea is that before we ever seek forgiveness for our sins, we are to have already forgiven those who have sinned against us. Jesus taught this principle in the parable of the unjust servant in Matthew 18:22-35. Human forgiveness is a reflection of God's forgiveness, and God' forgiveness avails for us only when we are willing to forgive one another. Jesus summarized these truths when He said: "And when ye stand praying, forgive, *if ye have ought against any; that your Father also which is in heaven may forgive you your trespasses. But if ye do not forgive, neither will your Father which is in heaven forgive your trespasses (Mark 11:25-26).*

Satan causes offenses in your family, between friends, in your business relationships, and in your church. The Bible states that offenses will come (Matt. 18:7). How will you deal with these issues when they arise? Will you intercede in prayer or just gossip about them?

In the Sermon on the Mount, Christ taught that we should love our enemies and pray for them. Jesus said: "Ye have heard that it hath been said, "Thou shall love thy neighbor, and hate thine enemy; But I say unto you, "Love your enemies, bless them that curse you, do good to them that hate you, and pray for them which despitefully use you, and persecute you; that ye may be the children of your Father in heaven (Matt. 5:43-45).

Ask yourself a question: How often have you spent time in prayer for your enemies, those who betrayed your confidences, lied about you, and hurt you deeply? Yet Jesus emphasized the importance of this type of prayer.

It is not difficult to pray for friends, family, and other believers in need, but praying for our enemies is not easy and cannot be done in the natural because it originates in the Father's heart. Only those who are truly His sons and daughters, born of His Spirit, can follow His example of love and forgiveness.

Jesus was despised, rejected, and betrayed even by those closest to Him. He was falsely accused, spit upon, made a public spectacle of shame and disgrace, and nailed to a cross. Hanging there, in pain and agony, Jesus prayed the greatest prayer ever prayed...*Father forgive the, for they know not what they do (Luke 23:34).* This prayer, falling from the lips of the Son of God, ascended unto the Father, who heard His cry, received the sacrifice of His life's blood, and responded by extending to man the priceless gift of salvation.

**And lead us not into temptation, but deliver us from evil:** Now Jesus taught us to pray, "Lead us not into temptation", but James indicates that God does not tempt man. *Let no man say when he is tempted, "I am tempted of God", for God cannot be tempted with evil, neither tempted he no man (James 1:13).*

The Bible reveals that tempting man is the role of our enemy, "Satan" (Matthew 4:3, 1 Thessalonians 3:5). The Bible also warns of temptations which come from the devil (Matthew 4:1, 1 Corinthians 7:5, and 1 Thessalonians 3:5). *When lust hath conceived, it bringeth forth sin: and sin, when it is finished, bringeth forth death (James 1:14-15).*

Satan is the tempter, but we are drawn into his snare when we allow our fleshly desires to entice us. Such desires birth sin and sin results in death. Some of Satan's attacks arise from uncontrolled evil passions from within, while other temptations come from our senses of hearing, seeing, feeling, touching, and tasting. Whatever their source, the apostle Paul assures us that: *There hath no temptation taken you but such as is common to man; but God is faithful, who will not suffer you to be tempted above that you are able, but will with the temptation also make a way to escape, that you will be able to bear it (1 Cor. 10:13)*. When we pray, "lead us not into temptation", we are asking God to preserve us from the enticement to sin. Even Jesus was not delivered from temptation, but was preserved in it (see Hebrews 4:15).

**For thine is the kingdom, and the power, and the glory forever:** The word "for" indicates the authority by which the Model Prayer has been prayed. It means "because" the kingdom, power, and glory belong to God, therefore, we can claim the provisions, promises, and protection of this prayer. When we arrive at this final portion of the Model Prayer and declare, thine is the kingdom, we are coming into agreement with everything God says about His Kingdom.

Here, the word for **power** is **dynamos,** from which the English words **"dynamic"** and **"dynamite"** come. When we end our prayer with thine is the power, we are acknowledging the dynamic power of God with its dynamite-like potential for fulfilling our petitions. When we declare, Thine is the power, God echoes back to us the words of Jesus, *"Behold, I give unto you power to tread on serpents and scorpions, and over all the power of the enemy; and nothing shall by any means hurt you (Luke 10:19).*

Thine is the **glory;** "Glory" is one of the richest words of the English language. No single words can serve as a good synonym, but here are some words that describe it: Honor, praise, splendor, radiance, power, exaltation, worthiness, likeness, beauty, renown, and rank. Jesus said: And the glory which thou gavest me I have given them; that they may be one even as we are one (John 17:22).

Now, this same glory which Jesus was glorified by the Father is a gift to you. All you must do is claim it. You should be going from glory to glory not from defeat to defeat. You may be discouraged, despondent, and feel cold and lifeless spiritually, but God's glory guarantees: Provision – Philippians 4:19, Ephesians 3:16; Strength – Colossians 1:11; Joy – Isaiah 66:5, 1 Peter 1:8 and 2 Chronicles 16:10; Liberty – Isaiah 60:1; Rest – Isaiah 11:10; Sanctification – Exodus 29:43, and Unity with other believers – John 17:22.

**"Forever"** means exactly what it says, *"eternal, having no end."* As you conclude your prayer by ascribing the kingdom, power, and glory to your Father forever, you are linking yourself in an eternal bond with Him as you acknowledge that you share in His kingdom, power, and glory.

**Amen:** When you use the word "Amen," it seals our prayer with powerful authority because Amen is one of the names of Christ (Revelation 3:14). Christ is called *"the Amen of God,"* for all of God's promises are fulfilled in Him. When we say amen, it means we have prayed all of our petitions in His Name.

The word amen does not mean over and out, and I'm done praying. The meaning of this word is: "Even so, as I have prayed it, even so shall it be done." So when you say amen, you are actually making a declaration of faith.

Remember, as you use the framework for your prayers, work for our prayers. It is not just a prayer to be repeated verbatim. It is an outline, given by our Lord, to provide the sequence and framework for our prayers. You can intercede for hours under just one point in the outline as the Holy Spirit empowers you to pray this prayer the way it was meant to be prayed.

# Nature and Significance of Prayer

Prayer is a significant and universal aspect of religion, whether of primitive peoples or of modern mystics that expresses the broad range of religious feelings and attitude that command man's relationship with the sacred or holy. Some have described prayer as a religious primary mode of expression. Prayer is said to be to religion what rational thought is to philosophy; it is the very expression of living religion.

Historians of religions, theologians, and believers of all faiths agree in recognizing the central position that prayer occupies in religion. According to American philosopher – without prayer there can be no question of religion. An Islamic proverb states that to pray and to be Muslim is synonymous. A modern Christian mystic of India, stated that praying is as important as breathing.

As we take a look of the various forms of religious literature, we find that prayer is considered by many to be the purest in expressing the essential elements of a religion. The Islamic Qur'an is regarded as a book of prayers, and the book of Psalms of the Bible is viewed as a meditation on biblical history turned into prayer. Some believed that if prayer were removed from the literary heritage of a culture, that culture would be deprived of a particularly rich and uplifting aspect.

From its primitive to its mystical expression, prayer expresses a desire on the part of men to enter into contact with the sacred or holy. Prayer is described here, not only as meditation about God but as a step, a going out of one' self, a pilgrimage of the spirit in the presence of God. It has therefore, a personal and experiential character that goes beyond critical analysis.

Prayer is also linked to sacrifice, which seems to support prayer as a cultic as well as a personal act, and as a supplement to the bare word of man in his attempts to relate to the sacred or holy. In many cases, the sacrificial act generally precedes the verbal act of prayer.

When prayer becomes dominating and manipulative in its intent, it becomes magic. With words and songs, man believes that he can ask, and threaten the sacred or supernatural power. The effectiveness of magical prayer is believed to depend on the recitation of a precise formula, or rhythm, or on the saying and repeating of the divine name. Manipulation by magic, however, is neither the explanation nor the essence of prayer but rather its deviation and exploitation, a tendency that is to be noticed whenever prayer departs from its basic and essential meaning – the expression of a desire to enter into contact with the sacred ore holy.

Some describe prayer as a subconscious and emotional effusion, an outburst of the mind that desires to enter into communication with the invisible. Experiences of prayer very often, in fact, do include, cries from the heart, inexpressible laments, and spiritual outburst.

Sociologists explain prayer in terms of the religious environment, which plays an indubitable role in spiritual behavior.

# The Lord's Prayer

The Lord's Prayer is a model for our prayers. It begins with adoration of God – acknowledges subjection to His will; asks petitions of Him, and ends with an ascription of praise.

**After this manner therefore pray ye, Our Father which art in heaven, Hallowed be thy name.** We notice here that the very beginning phrase, Our Father, is the first person of the Trinity – with one exception Jesus always spoke of God as the Father. The scripture identify the fatherhood of God in five areas. In James, He is the Father of Creation. In Jeremiah, He is the Father of Israel. In John He is the Father of Jesus. In Psalms, He is a protective Father emphasizing His defense of the poor and oppressed, and in Romans, He is a redemptive Father when we become the Children of God.

Just as our physical fathers provide many benefits, so our heavenly father also provides a number of spiritual benefits. Christians may have fellowship with the Father; they may have access with the Father; they receive guidance from the Father, and they get protection from God Our Father.

Now, just because God is the Father of us all, and because He is Father of Creation, does not necessary mean that everyone will go to heaven. A person must be born of God before he can become a Son of God. Then, God becomes a redemptive Father. Our Father is completely uncommon to the prayers of the Old Testament. Therefore, when our Lord says, Our Father, He was obviously thinking of Christian people, which means Christ-like – not those hypocrites, nor those so-called Christians.

Two major elements of the prayer are adoration and petition. Hallowed be thy name addresses the attention of the prayer toward God and reverence for this particular prayer closes with a doxology of praise **"for thine is the kingdom, and the power, and the glory, forever, Amen,** which is a liturgical interpolation from First Chronicles 29:11, which reads: *"Thine, O Lord, is the greatness, and the power, and the glory, and the victory, and the majesty: for all that is in the heaven and in the earth is thine; thine is the kingdom, O Lord, and thou are exalted as head above all.*

# *Biblical Men and Women who prayed*

**Cornelius** – A devout man and one who feared God with his entire house, which gave much alms to the people, and prayed to God always (Acts 10:2). And Cornelius said, "Four days ago I was fasting until this hour; and at the ninth hour I prayed in my house, and behold, a man stood before me in bright clothing" (Acts 10:30).

**Disciples Prays for Guidance:** According to Acts 1:24 – 25, the disciples chose a replacement for Judas. Two men, Joseph and Matthias met the established criterion which was that they must have accompanied the disciples during Ghrist's earthly ministry and must have been eyewitnesses to His resurrection. How would they choose between the two?

The disciples prayed that God would reveal His choice when they cast lots, which was an acceptable Old Testament method for guidance. And they prayed and said, *Thou, Lord which knowest the hearts of all men, shew whether of these two thou has chosen, that he may take part of this ministry and apostleship, from which Judas by transgression fell, that he might go to his own place. And they gave forth their lots; and the lot fell upon*

*Matthias, and he was numbered with the eleven apostles (Acts 1:24-26).*

It is important to note that this decision was made prior to the coming of the Holy Spirit. In every other case after the Spirit was given, the apostles sought guidance from the Holy Spirit. For an example, see Acts 13:1-13, where, through prayer and fasting, Barnabas and Paul were selected for mission outreaches. Never again in the Word of God was the casting of lots used to determine God's Will.

**Epaphras:** (Laboring in Prayer): In Paul's final remarks to the Colossians, he gives an update on several of his co-workers. One person Paul mentions, Epaphras, was the man who initially brought the Gospel to the Colossians. Epaphras was a fellow minister with Paul, and joined him in fervent prayer on behalf of the Colossian believers. Paul said; Epaphras, who is one of you and a servant of Christ Jesus, sends greetings. He is always wrestling in prayer for you, that you may stand firm in all the will of God, mature and fully assured (Colossians 4:12, NIV).

Epaphras was a praying pastor who labored fervently in prayer (wrestled), an expression from which the word "agony" comes. It is a term used for the extreme exertion of a wrestler. To labor or wrestle in prayer means, to pray earnestly, to struggle, and work hard. He prayed like a fighter.

In Paul's closing words to the Colossians, he said that Epaphras had prayed the God would help them to stand perfect and complete in all the will of God (Colossian 4:12). Now, the word perfect does not mean sinless – rather, it means fulfilled or mature. Epaphras had been praying that the Colossians might become all that they could be in Christ.

Sometimes prayer is not easy. Prayer can be difficult and tiring, but the results make it well worth the effort. Paus encourages us to continue in Prayer, setting Epaphras forth as an example of the kind of zealous praying that should characterize our prayers.

**Jairus** (Prayer in hopeless situation). This was the appeal of a man name Jairus who came to Jesus with a passionate request for his sick daughter (see Mark 5:23). Jesus agreed to accompany him, but on the way, another desperate person sought His attention. A woman with an incurable issue of blood was among the crowd following Him (Mark 5:27-29). When she heard that Jesus was coming, she pushed into the mob of people behind Him, reached out, and touched His garment – for she said, *"If I may touch but his clothes, I shall be whole. And straightway the fountain of her blood was dried up; and she felt in her body that she was healed of the plague (Mark 5:28-29).* The portion of Christ's garment that many biblical scholars believe she touched was the threads of the tallit, symbolizing the promises of God.

Jesus called the woman out of the crowd, and declared, *daughter, thy faith hath made thee whole; go in peace, and be whole of thy plague (Mark 5:34).* While He paused to deal with this situation, a servant came from Jairus house with bad news. His daughter was dead, as he said, and it was not necessary to trouble Jesus any further. If Jairus had listened to this report, he would have stopped before getting his miracle.

Jesus told Jairus to be not afraid, only believe. Then, taking Peter, James, and John, Jesus cleared the room of those who were mourning, took the young girl's hand and commanded the damsel to arise, (Mark 5:41), and immediately, the girl was restored back to life.

These were two hopeless situations. One had an incurable illness; the other was dead. In both instances Jesus inspired faith. Your faith has made you whole. Do not fear, only believe! And in both instances, the miracle answer came.

Don't retreat in the face of hopeless situations. Take your impossible circumstances to Jesus. Reach out by faith to touch Him. Grab hold, and don't let go. No matter what impossibilities you face, no matter how others try to discourage you, don't give up. Do not fear. Only believe.

Bring your hopeless situation to Jesus as tenaciously as Jairus brought his daughter to Him. Bring those who are lost and dying in sin for a touch of the Master's hand. Grab hold of the promises of God as the woman with the issue of blood took hold of Christ's garment. Don't let go, and don't give up.

**Jesus Christ** – (A model prayer life). Jesus Christ is our greatest model of intercessory prayer – The most powerful person in prayer of any in biblical record. He began His ministry with prayer at His baptism (Luke 3:21), and enable it with prayer on the Cross (Matthew chapter 27).

Jesus made it a regular habit to devote the early hours of the day to prayer (Mark 1:35, John 7:16-18, 8:29, 12:49). He lived in the spirit of prayer. He prayed in every emergency, in every situation, and at every opportunity. He prayed in the midst of a busy schedule, to escape popularity, and after ministry successes. Jesus prayed for His friends (Luke 22:32, John 11:41-42), His followers (John Chapter 17), and His enemies (Luke 23:34).

**Jesus made prayer a priority:** He prayed any time of the day or night (Luke 6:12-13). Prayer took priority over eating and over business (John 4:31-32). He taught prayer to His disciple in Matthew 6:9-13.

**Jesus prays in Gethsemane:** Here, the Garden of Gethsemane was the setting for one of the most intense prayers ever prayed by our Lord. Jesus was overwhelmed with sorrow as He faced His forthcoming arrest and death, so He asks His disciples to tarry with Him in prayer (Matthew 26:37-38).

In Gethsemane, Jesus drew apart from the disciples, fell on His face and prayed, *O my Father, if it be possible, let this cup pass from me: nevertheless not my will, but as thou will (Matthew 26;39).* It was a cry that came from the depths of His being. The word "Abba" is only used three times in the Bible, and this is the only record we have of Jesus using it in personal prayer. It is an Aramaic word denoting deep intimacy and the term used for "Father or Daddy". It was a word the Jews didn't use to address God because they thought it was disrespectful. In His hour of greatest agony, however, Jesus used this intimate term of endearment to cry out to His Father.

After Jesus returned to check on His disciples, He found them sleeping. Not only did they miss the significance of this prayer time, but also they failed to prepare themselves for the testing that lay ahead. He warned them to *Watch and pray that ye enter not into temptation; the spirit indeed is willing, but the flesh is weak (Matthew 26:41).*

Now, Gethsemane means "Olive oil press", after the device by which olives are crushed under the weight of a stone to obtain their oil. Jesus was being crushed by the weight of the Father's will; for He was to carry the load of our sin and shame. Three times Jesus asked God if He might be delivered from His assignment, and three times He added, *not my will, but thine will be done (Luke 22:42).* Sometimes the only way for a cup of difficulty to pass is to drink from it, fully confident that God will help you through it. When faced with difficulties where you aren't sure how to pray, just surrender your will to God and say, not my will, Lord, but let your will be done.

Let us imagine Christ, there in the Garden. Beneath Him on the ground is the crimson red of the mixture of His blood with His tears. He agonized and travailed in prayer until His sweat became drops of blood: And being in agony he prayed more earnestly; and the sweat was as it were great drops of blood falling down to the ground (Luke 22:44).

Isaiah prophesied, *yet it pleased the Lord to bruise him; he hath put him to grief; when thou shalt make his soul an offering for sin (Isaiah 53:10). The Lord hath laid on him the iniquity of us all (Isaiah 53:6). He shall see of the travail of his soul, and shall be satisfied by his knowledge shall my righteous servant justify many; for he shall bear their iniquities (Isaiah 53:11).*

Jesus was about to taste death for every man (Hebrews 2:9). He was going to bear the curse and suffer the wages of sin for all mankind. Jesus was in agony because He knew that His Father could not look upon sin and would have to turn away from Him for a time. He didn't want to break His fellowship with the Father.

Hebrews 5:7-9 lets me know that His prayer was heard by God: *Who in the days of his flesh, when he had offered up prayers and supplications with strong crying and tears unto him that was able to save him from death, and was heard in that he feared; though he were a Son, yet learned his obedience by the things which he suffered; The battle for the souls of mankind was won there in the Garden, and on the cross - Jesus*, being made perfect, he became the author of eternal salvation unto all mankind.

**Prayer accompanied every important event in His life.** Prayer at His baptism (Luke 3:21-22) – During His first ministry tour (Mark 1:35, Luke 5:16) – Before His choice of the disciples – (Luke 6:12-13) – Before and after feeding the five thousand (Matthew 14:19-23, Mark 6:41- 46 and John 6:11, 14-15) – At the feeding of the four thousand (Matt. 15:36, Mark 8:6,7) – Before Peter's confession (Luke 9:20) – Before the transfiguration (Luke 9:28-29) – At the return of the Seventy (Matt. 11:25, Luke 10:17-21) – At Lazarus grave (John 11:41,42) – At the blessing of the children (Matt. 19:13) – At the coming of certain Greeks (John 12:2728) – For Peter (Luke 22:32) – For the giving of the Holy Spirit (John14:16) – On the road to Emmaus (Luke 24:30-31) – Prior to His ascension (Luke 24:50-53) – For His followers, John 17 – Before His trial (Matthew 26:26-27; Mark 14:22-23; Luke 22:17-19), and on the Cross (Matt. 27:46; Mark 15:34, and Luke 23:34-46).

**Jesus prayed that the Father might be glorified:** Jesus prays regarding His forthcoming death. First, He said: *The hour is come, that the Son of man should be glorified. Verily, verily, I* *say unto you, except a corn of wheat fall into the ground and die, it abideth alone; but if it dies, it bringeth forth much fruit. He that loveth his life shall lose it; and he that hateth his life in this world shall keep it unto life eternal (John 12:23-25).* Jesus knew that in order to save many lives, He must sacrifice His own life. He said:

*"Now is my soul troubled and what shall I say? (John 12:27).* No wonder He was troubled – He was facing torture and ultimate death by one of the most cruel, inhumane methods of the known world. Yet He prayed; *Father, save me from this hour; but for this cause came I unto this hour. Father, glorify thy name. Then came there a voice from heaven, saying, I have both glorified it, and will glorify it again (John 12:27-28).*

Jesus knew what lay ahead of Him. His own desire was to be saved from it, but He realized that this was the whole purpose of His earthly existence, so He resigned His will to the Father's Will. His main concern was that God be glorified. In answer to His prayer, the Father spoke from heaven and said, *I have both glorified it, and will glorify it again (John 12:28)*

When facing the darkest experience of His life, Jesus was more concerned that the Father be glorified than He was about His own suffering. When you are facing difficult times, how do you pray? Most likely, you cry for help and deliverance, and that is normal. But next time, why not change your focus. Realize that everything that happens isn't about you, but it is about God's purposes being fulfilled. Instead of complaining, moaning, or groaning about your circumstances, pray that God will be glorified.

**Jesus prays to His Father to glorify him, and for restoration.**
(His intercessory and farewell prayer). *These words spake Jesus, and lifted up his eyes to heaven, and said,*

*"Father, the hour is come; glorify thy Son, that thy Son also may glorify thee. As thou has given him power over all flesh, that he should give eternal life to as many as thou has given him. And this is life eternal, that they might know thee the only true God and Jesus Christ, whom thou has sent. I have glorified thee on the earth; I have finished the work which thou gavest me to do. And now, O Father, glorify thou me with thine own self with the glory, which I had with thee before the world was (St. John 17:1-5).*

**He prayed a special prayer for the church**. *I pray for them; I pray not for the world, but for them which thou hast given me; for they are thine, and all mine are thine, and thine are mine; and I am glorified in them (St. John 17:9-10).*

**He prays for the keeping of the saints**. *And now I am no more in the world, but these are in the world, and I come to thee, Holy Father, keep through thine own name those whom thou hast given me, that they may be one, as we are (St. John 17:11).*

**Jesus prays that the church may be kept pure.** *I pray not that thou shouldest take them out of the world, but that thou shouldest keep them from the evil. They are not of the world, even as I am not of the world. Sanctify them through thy truth: thy word is truth (St. John 17:15-17).*

**Jesus prays for the unity of the church.** *That they all may be one; as thou Father, art in me, and I in thee, that theyalso may be one in us: that the world may believe that thou hast sent me (St. John 17:21).*

**He prays for sending the Comforter.** *And I will* pray the Father, and he shall give you another comforter, that he may abide with you *forever (St John 14:16).*

**Jesus prays at His Baptism:** After Jesus was baptized He came up out of the muddy waters of the Jordan River and began to pray. *Now when all the people were baptized, it came to pass, that Jesus also being baptized, and praying, the heaven was opened, and the Holy Ghost descended in a bodily shape like a dove upon Him, and a voice came from heaven which said, Thou art my beloved Son; in thee I am well pleased (St. Luke 3:21-22).* Standing there, with water streaming down His face and pouring off His body, Jesus began to commune with God, to surrender Himself totally to the plan and purpose God had for His life.

Jesus had a vibrant, living relationship with the Father. Through prayer, He lived in constant communion with God. He would often rise up early in the morning and go to a solitary place to pray. After times of intense teaching and ministry to the people, He would find a place where He could be alone with the Father. It was during these times alone in prayer that Jesus maintained an intimate relationship with the Father, where He could say, *As the Father knoweth me, even so know I the Father (St. John 10:15).*

Although Jesus was the Son of God, His knowledge of and relationship with the Father was not automatic. He was in the form of human flesh, and it was necessary for Him to learn the things God wanted Him to say and do. It was necessary for Him to draw strength from His Father.

Jesus did nothing independently of His Father, only those things that were revealed to Him by the Father. How was it possible for Jesus, who was in the form of human flesh, like you and me, to enter the realm of the Spirit and see what the Father was doing? How did God reveal to Jesus the words He was to speak and the things He was to do through prayer? Jesus lived in a vital union with God where He and the Father were one. He could say, the Father is in me, and I in Him (St. John 10:38); I and my Father are one (St. John 10:30), because He lived in a powerful dimension of the Spirit in prayer where the Father fully revealed His will. Through prayer Jesus was able to see in the Spirit the things the Father wanted Him to do. Through prayer Jesus was able to heal in the Spirit the words the Father wanted Him to speak.

As Jesus prayed and talked with the Father, the Father made Himself known in all His fullness. He revealed His character, love, mercy, and power. He revealed His will to save, heal, deliver, and set men free from Satan's power. As He saw these things in the Spirit through prayer, He did them. He told the Jews, that *the Son can do nothing of himself, but what he seeth the Father do (St. John 5:19).* Therefore whatever Jesus saw the Father do, He did also.

It was through prayer that Jesus was able to penetrate into the realm of the Spirit. It was through prayer that the Father revealed Himself and His will to Jesus. This knowledge of God, which Jesus gained through prayer, was the foundation of all He said and did.

Therefore, in order to become a powerful end-time spiritual warrior, you must also come into a position where you know God and are one with Him, where you can see and hear in the Spirit. One of God's purposes for your life is for you to grow spiritually until you come into the full knowledge of the Son of God. There is only one way that you will be able to do this, and that is through prayer. Just as it was necessary for Jesus, in the form of human flesh, to use prayer as a means of communicating with God and knowing His will, it is necessary for you to use prayer as a means of coming into the full and accurate knowledge of Jesus.

Whatever your time commitment to prayer is right now, increase it. The demands on your time may be great, but you must not allow this to crowd out your time alone with Christ. As Jesus begins to reveal Himself and His will to you during these times of prayer, you will come into a greater knowledge of who He is and who you are as a child of the living God.

**Jesus prays before calling the twelve Apostles.** Jesus spent the entire night in prayer prior to selecting the disciples who were to become the foundation stones in the church. The choice would have eternal consequences. Upon their shoulders would rest the future of the Gospel, and most of them would be called upon to forfeit their lives for the sake of the Gospel. *And it came to pass in those days, that he went out into a mountain to pray, and continued all night in prayer to God. And when it was day, He called unto Him His disciples; and of them he chose twelve, whom also he named apostles (Luke 6:12-13).*

When looking on the list of those chosen, it is doubtful that they would have been selected from an earthly viewpoint - Simple fishermen - A tax collector and uneducated men. All would desert Him some day. One would deny Him. One would ultimately betray Him; yet, all were chosen within the Will of God.

Nevertheless, God said in Isaiah 55:8-9 that: *For my thoughts are not your thoughts, neither are your ways my ways, saith the Lord. For as the heavens are higher than the earth, so are my ways higher than your ways, and my thoughts than your thoughts.*

We notice here that God's choice does not always agree with what we would choose in the natural. That is why it's so important to earnestly pray regarding our decisions. Making good decisions isn't always the result of a quick prayer. Time and intensity are often necessary to make wise choices within the Will of God.

**Jesus prays at Mount of Olives for weak believers** – *But I have prayed for thee, that thy faith fail not; and when thou art converted, strengthen thy brethren. And when he was at the place, he said unto them, pray that ye enter not into temptation. And he was withdrawn from them about a stone's cast, and kneeled down, and prayed, saying, Father, if thou be willing, remove this cup from me; nevertheless not my will, but thine, be done. And there appeared an angel unto Him from heaven, strengthening Him. And being in an agony He prayed more earnestly; and His sweat was as it were great drops of blood falling down to the ground (Luke 22:32-40, 40-44).*

**Jesus prays at His Transfiguration:** *And as he prayed, the fashion of his countenance was altered, and his raiment was white and glistering (Luke 9:29).*

**Jesus prays before the Agony of the Cross:** *And He went a little further, and fell on his face, and prayed, saying, O my Father, if it be possible, let this cup pass from me: Nevertheless not as I will, but as thou will. He went again the second time, and prayed saying, O my Father, if this cup may not pass away* from me, except I drink it, they will be done. And He left them, and went away again, and prayed the third time, saying the same words (Matthew 26:39, 42, 44). And He went forward a little, and fell on the ground; and prayed that, if it were possible, the hour might pass from Him. And again He went and prayed and spoke the same words (Mark 14:35, 39).

**Jesus prays in the morning** – *And in the morning, rising up a great while before day, he went out and departed into a solitary place, and prayed (Mark 1:35).*

**Jesus prays in the evening:** *And when He had sent them away, He departed into a mountain to pray. And when evening was come, the ship was in the midst of the sea, and he alone on the land (Mark 6:46-47.*

**Jesus Prays all night** – *And it came to pass in those days, that He went out into a mountain to pray, and continued all night in prayer to God (Luke 6:12).*

**Jesus goes to a solitary place to communicate with the Father** – *But so much the more went there a fame abroad of Him; and great multitude came together to hear, and to be healed by Him of their infirmities. And He withdrew Himself into the wilderness and prayed (Luke 5:15-16).*

**Jesus' proof in producing prayer:** Now the purpose of Jesus coming to earth was to destroy the works of the enemy, including sin, sickness and bondage. *For this purpose the Son of God was manifested, that He might destroy the works of the devil (1John 3:8).*

Although prayer is not specifically mentioned in all of the miracles performed by Jesus; it was His constant communication with God that produced the manifestation of signs and wonders. There are several references in the New Testament about Jesus healing everyone present. Jesus healed many types of diseases such as epilepsy, dropsy, the deaf and dumb, the paralyzed, those with chronic hemorrhaging, the demonized, the deformed, the blind, and those having various infirmities. He raised the dead and did miracles of restoration, such as attaching a detached ear.

Sometimes Jesus called the sick to Him (Mark 3:1-6). Other times they called for Him (Matthew 8:5-13, 9:18-19, 9:23-26, and Luke 7:1-10). Jesus dealt with the whole man, not just the physical condition. He taught forgiveness of sin and healing together. Sometimes He healed first, then forgave sin (Luke 17:9 and John 5:14). Other times He forgave sin first, then healed (Mark 2:1-12).

Sometimes Jesus would even combine a prayer command of faith and touch, as in the case of the leper in Matthew 8:2-4; the two blind men in Matthew 9:27-31; Peter's mother-in-law in Luke 4:38-39; the deaf and dumb man in Mark 7:32-35; the widow's son in Luke 7:12-15, and the daughter of Abraham in Luke 13:10-13

Sometimes Jesus prayed, as in the cases of Peter's mother-in-law; the deaf and dumb man; the widow's son; Lazarus in John 11:38-44, and the man with a withered hand in Mark 3:1-5. Whether prayer was mentioned or not, we know from the Gospels that everything Jesus did, said, or taught was saturated in prayer.

**Praying for the Harvest:** Jesus left only one prayer request for His church: *"But when He saw the multitudes, he was moved with compassion on them, because they fainted, and were scattered abroad, as sheep having no shepherd. Then saith He unto His disciples, the harvest truly is plenteous, but the laborers are few; Pray ye therefore the Lord of the harvest, that He will send forth laborers into His harvest (Matthew 9:36-38).*

Effective prayer for spiritual harvest must flow from a heart of compassion. Jesus was moved with compassion when He saw the needs of the people. It was from this compassion that the request emanated.

Effective prayer for spiritual harvest involves prayer for the deployment of laborers and the reaping of souls. We must pray for a harvest of souls as well as for laborers to reap it.

Effective prayer for spiritual harvest involves our willingness to respond. When we pray this prayer, it is an indication of our own willingness to be part of the answer. Not long after praying this, the disciples are commissioned and sent as laborers (Matthew 10:1). The very ones Jesus commissioned to pray for laborers became harvesters themselves.

**Jesus prays on the cross for His enemies.** *Then said Jesus, Father, forgive them; for they know not what they do. And they parted His raiment, and cast lots (Luke 23:34). And He kneeled down, and cried with a loud voice; Lord, lay not this sin to their charge. And when He had said this, He felled asleep (Acts 7:60).*

**Jesus' prayer on the cross:** Jesus lifted three prayers during the terrible ordeal on the cross. **The first prayer** was, *Father, forgive them, for they know not what they do (Luke 23:34).*

Despite the pain, suffering, and humiliation, Jesus prayed for those who were responsible. He interceded for them, asking that God would forgive them.

**The second prayer lifted by Jesus was:** *My God, my God, why hast thou forsaken me? (Matt. 27:46 and Mark 15:34).* While experiencing the awful darkness, the physical agony, and the sense of separation from God, Jesus lifted this anguished cry. The prayer, though only a short sentence must have torn the heart of God. But to complete redemption's plan, the Father had to allow His Son to pass through those dreadful moments. This prayer is actually a quote from Psalm 22, which begins with despair but ends with hope and describes Christ's experience on the Cross.

**The third prayer Jesus prayed on the Cross was very brief;** *Father, into thy hands I commend my spirit (Luke 23:46).* Despite His pain, humiliation, and the temporary alienation from God, He still entrusted His spirit into the hands of the Father.

From these examples, we learn that we can pray like Jesus in the midst of our own suffering. We can pour out our anguish, confessing God's sovereignty, even as we acknowledge the pain we are experiencing, and we can commit ourselves and our circumstances into His loving care.

**John the Revelator** – The Isle of Patmos lies about thirty seven miles southwest of Miletus in the Mediterranean Sea. It is about ten miles long and six miles wide at the north end and consists mainly of volcanic hills and rocky ground. In the New Testament times it was a desolate island used by the Romans to exile prisoners.

It was in the year 95 A.D., during the reign of the Roman Emperor Domitian, that the Apostle John was exiled here for his faith in God. This was no tropical paradise. It was a lonely, deserted, barren place. But, it was the Lord's Day, and despite the fact that John was alone and in desperate circumstances, he decided to worship God. Little did John realize that this worship experience would not only dramatically transform his own life, it would impact generations to come and affect the destiny of the entire world.

*John was in the spirit on this Lord's Day, as he received the revelation of Jesus Christ, which God gave unto him, to shew unto His servants things which must shortly come to pass, and He sent and signified it by his angel unto His servant John (Revelation 1:1).*

This powerful revelation came to John in one of the darkest times of his life, as he was exiled on this lonely Island. Divine revelation often comes in difficult times. It was in exile that Jacob saw God at Bethel (Genesis 35:1). It was in exile that Elijah heard the voice of God (1 kings 19:3-9). It was in exile that Ezekiel saw the glory of the Lord (Ezekiel 1:3). It was in exile that Daniel saw his vision of God (Daniel 7:9).

If you are going through a difficult time in your life, you can succumb to a depression of pity, or you – like the Apostle John, can get in the Spirit and begin to worship God. Reflect for a moment, what God may be trying to birth through you or reveal to you in your darkest hour: Begin to worship Him, and divine revelation will come.

**Mary (Her passionate praise).** In Matthew 26:6-13, Mary carefully held the fragile alabaster bottle in her hands, fingering it lovingly. Inside the bottle was spikenard, perfume she had saved for the future. Mary slowly opened the bottle to smell the beautiful fragrance. As she looked at the alabaster bottle, she remembered the sacrifices that had been made to buy it. It was her most valuable possession, worth 300 denaridenarii, which was the equivalent to a man's wages for an entire year.

Mary hesitated for a moment, and then made her way to where Jesus was visiting with his friends. Mary knelt at Jesus' feet, broke the alabaster bottle, and began to pour the contents over His feet. She had heard Jesus say that He was going to be crucified, and she couldn't bear the thought. Her heart was overflowing with love for her Lord and Master. Tears flowed down her face and mingled with the perfumes as she washed His feet. Then she unwound her long black hair and used it to dry His feet wit – expressing her passionate, extravagant love for Him.

As Mary anointed Jesus' feet, and the beautiful aroma of the spikenard filled the room, Judas Iscariot looked on with disgust. He considered this lavish expression of love a waste and wanted Jesus to rebuke her. Those who walk in the Spirit always anger those who walk in the flesh. The room grew quiet as they waited for Jesus' response. Jesus said; let her alone. What she is doing now is in preparation for the day of my burial. *For ye have the poor always with you; but me ye have not always (Matthew 26:11).*

This story is one of the greatest illustrations of passionate worship in the Bible. Mary sacrificed her most valuable possession in an act of lavish worship, and she is a stellar example of the type of worshippers God is seeking. Worshippers like Abraham, who was willing to sacrifice his only son. Worshippers like Job, who bowed before God when he had lost all. Worshippers like King

David, who declared he would not offer God a sacrifice that did not cost him something.

Worship is a powerful practice that brings down God's glory and puts the enemy to flight; yet there is a general lack of understanding concerning it. For the most part, worship has been relegated to a designated time when the choir sings and the worship team leads people in a few songs. The pattern is usually to start with a couple of un-beat, fast-paced songs and then move to a slower, more worshipful song to prepare for the sermon. In many churches, the worship music has become more entertainment-oriented and the singers more performance-oriented than worship-oriented.

Singing, dancing, shouting, and rejoicing are all a part of worship, but they must not become the focal point. Having our emotions stirred is not enough. Jesus told the Samaritan woman at Jacob's well: *But the hour cometh, and now is, when the true worshippers shall worship the Father in spirit and in truth: for the Father seeketh such to worship him. God is a Spirit: and they that worship him must worship him in spirit and in truth (John 4:23-24).*

True praise and worship does not originate from the soul – the mind, will, and emotions. True worship originates in the spirit. Worship is not some dead, dry, formal routine based upon man-made traditions. It is not an emotional high that we must work up. The worship that reaches the heart of the Father is done in the Spirit. It is an expression or passionate love, praise, and adoration from the heart that is directed to God.

A sovereign move of God is coming to the Church whereby He will bring forth a pure stream of worship, as believers embrace this new dimension of worship where they are no longer bound by tradition but are unreservedly worshipping God with all of their heart, God's glory will descend. The heavens will open, and there, in the holy atmosphere of God's presence, intercessors will be able to boldly stand before the throne and intercede on behalf of people groups and nations.

Now, the Greek word for worship is proskyneo, meaning, "to prostrate oneself, do reverence to, to ascribe worth." It denotes adoration, and act of rendering divine honor, esteem, and love. When we worship the Father and Jesus, we pour out our love for who they are, rather than what they have done for us.

The Bible says, *He who brings an offering of praise and thanksgiving honors and glorifies me (Psalms 50: 23, AMP).* Thanksgiving, like praise, draws the heart away from self and centers it upon God. This is why, when we come before God in prayer, we should begin by giving thanks, praise, and worship before we present our needs.

In a world where many worship power, money, sex, and pleasure, God is searching for true worshipers. He seeks those who will build a living memorial to Him through worship, like Mary, who poured our extravagant worship on the Lord Jesus. Many believers have placed their families, careers, and the pursuit of pleasure first in their lives, and these things have become their idols. There are others who have put ministry above the Lord, and it has become their god. They are too busy in their word for the Lord to take time for the Lord.

God has made us a royal priesthood to proclaim His praises to the end of the earth. *But ye are a chosen generation, a royal priesthood, an holy nation, a peculiar people; that ye should shew forth the praises of him who hath called you out of darkness into his marvelous light (1 Peter 2:9).*

Something happens in the spirit realm when God's people begin to truly worship Him. There is a release in the spirit, and new freedom comes forth. The shackles of fear, doubt, and worry begin to break, and Satan is defeated.

**Worship, Praise, and Thanksgiving** are vitally linked in prayer. In fact, they are inseparable. The Apostle Paul said, Continue in prayer, and watch in the same with thanksgiving; (Colossians 4:2). Writing to the Thessalonians, he again links prayer and thanksgiving: *Rejoice evermore. Pray without ceasing. In everything give thanks; for this is the will of God in Christ Jesus concerning you (1 Thessalonians 5:16-18).* To the Philippians he wrote: *Be careful for nothing; but in everything by prayer and supplication with thanksgiving; let your requests be made known unto God (Philippians 4:6).*

We must not be bound by man's traditions, and not limit worship only to the times set aside in church gatherings. Let your worship be spontaneous. Paul told the Ephesians: *But be filled with the Spirit; speaking to yourselves in psalms and hymns and spiritual songs, singing and making melody in your heart to the Lord: (Ephesians 5:18-19).*

Then when Mary was come where Jesus was, and saw him, she fell down at his feet, saying unto Him, Lord, if thou had been here, my brother had not died.

**Paul – (The Apostle of Prayer):** One of the greatest examples of an intercessor in the Bible is the Apostle Paul. From his conversion until his death, his life was saturated with prayer.

Paul's divine encounter on the road to Damascus totally transformed his life (See Acts Chapter 9). He saw the glorified Christ and was a changed man from that day forward. The very first thing he did after this glorious encounter was to spend three days in prayer and fasting to await further instructions from the Lord concerning what He wanted him to do.

During Paul's encounter with the Lord, he was three *days without sight (Acts 9:9)*. Although he could not see with his physical eyes, the Lord gave him spiritual vision. As he prayed and fasted, he had a vision of a man named Ananias coming to Judas's house (where Paul was staying), placing his hands on him and praying for his eyes to be healed. At the same time, the Lord appeared to Ananias in a vision and directed him to go to go into the street which is called Straight, and inquire in the house of Judas for one called Saul (Paul), of Tarsus; *for, behold, he prayeth (Acts 9:11)*.

Ananias obeyed the Lord, came to the house, laid his hands on Paul, and said: *"Brother Saul, the Lord, even Jesus that appeared unto thee in the way as thou camest has sent me that thou mightiest receive thy sight, and be filled with the Holy Ghost" (Acts 9:17)*. Immediately, Paul's eyes were healed. Something like scales fell from his eyes, and he could see again. He rose up and was baptized.

Paul spent several days with the disciples in Damascus, preaching and teaching in the synagogue, and then he went to Arabia, where he spent time alone with the Lord. Paul said: *Immediately I conferred not with flesh and blood: neither went I up to Jerusalem to them which were apostles before me; but I went into Arabia, and returned again unto Damascus.*

I don't recall the Bible saying how much time Paul spent in Arabia, but is evident that Paul's priority was to sit at the feet of Jesus, receive revelation, and be empowered by Him. Paul received and shared a powerful revelation from the Lord regarding the divine energizing of the Holy Ghost in prayer. *Likewise the Spirit also helps our infirmities: for we know not what we should pray for as we ought, but the Spirit itself maketh intercession for us with groaning's which cannot be uttered (Romans 8:26).*

Paul learned by revelation how to pray with power. He recognized that he did not know how to pray, but entered a new dimension of prayer whereby the Holy Ghost prayed through him on behalf of believers. Paul taught by revelation knowledge what he learned at the feet of Jesus about spiritual warfare, saying: *For we wrestle not against flesh and blood, but against principalities, against powers, against the rulers of the darkness of this world, against spiritual wickedness in high places (Ephesians 6:12).*

Through experience, Paul learned the power of prayer in spiritual warfare and in pulling down strongholds: *Tor the weapons of our warfare are not carnal, but mighty through God to the pulling down of strong holds; Casting down imaginations, and every high thing that exalteth itself against the knowledge of God, and bringing into captivity every thought to the obedience of Christ (2 Corinthians 10:4-5).*

Paul learned firsthand how to confront the enemy, engage him in one-on-one combat, and defeat him. He was not just teaching theory or his own ideas. He imparted by revelation knowledge what the Holy Spirit revealed and manifested in his life. Now, let's take a look at Paul's testimony to the believers in Corinth. He said: *And I, brethren when I came to you, came not with Excellency of speech or of wisdom, declaring unto you the testimony of God. For I determined not to know anything among you, save Jesus Christ and him crucified (1 Corinthians 2:1-2).*

Paul was not depending on man's wisdom but on the power of the Holy Ghost. He said *my speech and my preaching was not with enticing words of man's wisdom, but in demonstration of the Spirit and of power: (1 Corinthians 2:4). He said, we speak not in the words which man's wisdom teacheth, but which the Holy Ghost teacheth; comparing spiritual things with spiritual (1 Corinthians 2:13).*

Everything Paul did was born in prayer, sustained in prayer, and accomplished through prevailing prayer: When Paul went on his first missionary trip, it was under the power of prayer and fasting: *As they ministered to the Lord, and fasted, the Holy Ghost said, Separate me Barnabas and Saul for the work whereunto I have called them. And when they had fasted and prayed, and laid their hands on them, they sent them away (Acts 13:2-3).*

When Paul began his ministry in Philippi, he started it in a prayer meeting on the side of the river: *And on the Sabbath we went out of the city by a river side, where prayer was wont to be made; and we sat down, and spake unto the women which resorted thither (Acts 16:13).*

Every church that Paul established was through prayer and fasting: *And when they had ordained them elders in every church, and had prayed with fasting, they commended them to the Lord, on whom they believed (Acts 14:23).*

Because Paul lived in continual communion with God, supernatural power flowed out of him: And God wrought special miracles by the hands of Paul: So that from his body were brought unto the sick handkerchiefs or aprons, and the diseases departed from them, and the evil spirits went out of them (Acts 19:1-12).

Paul was a man of faith, revelation, and power because he was above all else – a man of prayer. Throughout his Epistles we have a picture of a man whose teaching on prayer could be summed up with his own words, *Pray without ceasing (1 Thessalonians 5:17).*

Now, let's take a brief spiritual journey through the churches Paul established and look at the example of prayer he set. **(1) To the church in Rome,** Paul wrote: *For God is my witness, whom I serve with my spirit in the gospel of His Son, that without ceasing I make mention of you always in my prayers; making request, if by any means now at length I might have a prosperous journey by the will of God to come unto you. For I long to see you, that I may impart unto you some spiritual gift, to the end ye may be established (Romans 1:9-11).*

Paul prayed apostolic prayers without ceasing on behalf of the believers in Rome. The great cry of his heart was that they would grow in the grace of God and become firmly established. **(2) To the church in Corinth,** he wrote: *I thank my God always on your behalf, for the grace of God which given you by Jesus Christ; (1 Corinthians 1:4).* He urged them to seek spiritual gifts. He said, *I will pray with the spirit, and I will pray with the understanding also (1 Corinthians 14:15). I thank my God, I speak with tongues more than ye all do (1 Cor. 14:18).* He gave himself as an example to follow in ministry: *But in* *all things approving ourselves as the ministers of God, in much patience, in afflictions, in necessities, in distresses, in stripes, in imprisonment's, in tumults, in labours, in watching, in fasting; (2 Corinthians 6:4-5).* **(3) To the church in Galatia:** Paul told the believers that he travailed in prayer on their behalf. He said, *my little children, of whom travail in birth again until Christ be formed in you (Galatians 4:19).*

The word travail is translated from a Hebrew word, which means, ***"to writhe in pain."*** It is compared with the indescribable pain a woman experiences in the last stages of labor, before giving birth to her child. Travailing in prayer involves a deep level of intensity, a groaning in the Spirit, and agonizing and wrestling in prayer. Travailing prayer goes beyond ordinary prayer, it is when the Holy Spirit takes over and begins to pray through us with groaning too deep for words. **(4) To the church in Ephesus:** Paul told the Ephesians, *cease not to give thanks for you, making mention of you in my prayers, (Ephesians 1:16). For this cause I bow my knees unto the Gather of our Lord Jesus Christ that he would grant you, according to the riches of his glory, to be strengthened with might by his Spirit in the inner man: (Eph. 3:14,16).* **(5) To the church in Philippi:** Paul said, *I thank my God upon every remembrance of you, always in every prayer of mine for you all making request with joy (Philippians 1:3-4). For God is my record, how greatly I long after you all in the bowels of Jesus Christ. And this I pray (Philippians 1:8-9).* **(6) To the church in Colossian:** Paul told the believers that he prayed without ceasing for them. He said, we give thanks to God, praying always for you, for this cause we also, since the day we heard it, do not cease to pray for you (Colossians 1:3,9). I would that ye knew what great conflict I have for you, and for as many as have not seen my face in the flesh (Colossians 2:1). **(7) To the church in Thessalonica:**

Paul said, *we give thanks to God always for you all, making mention of you in our prayers (1 Thessalonians 1:2).* He told them that he was praying exceedingly for them. *For what thanks can we render to God again for you, for all the joy wherewith we joy for your sakes before our God; night and day praying exceedingly that we might see your face, and might perfect that which is lacking in your faith? (1 Thessalonians 3:9, 10). We are bound to thank God always for you, brethren, as it is meet, because that your faith growth exceedingly, and the charity of every one of you all toward each other aboundeth; wherefore also we pray always for you, that our God would count you worthy of this calling, and fulfill all the good pleasure of his goodness, and the work of faith with power (2 Thessalonians 1:3, 11)*Paul apostolic prayers helped establish the church on a strong foundation and made it a powerful force against which the gates of hell could not prevail. Paul apostolic prayers also revealed that he carried a very deep prayer burden for the Jews. He said: *My heart's desire and prayer to God for Israel is that they might be saved (Romans 10:1).* I have great heaviness and continual sorrow in my heart. For I could wish that myself were accursed from Christ for my brethren (Romans 9:2-3).

Paul gave himself continually to prayer. He believed that prayer should be the life flow of the Church. He taught that we are to pray everywhere, in every situation, and without ceasing. He was definitely an example of a man who was powerful in prayer.

What we need in the Church today is a revival of apostolic praying. Just as God used Paul's prayers to build a strong foundation for the Early Church, we need anointed men and women of God to pray apostolic prayers that will bring the church to full maturity. We need Christian leaders who are willing to pay the price by giving themselves in unceasing prayer, as Paul did, so that believers will rise up in the anointing of power to fulfill God's mandate in this end-time hour.

**His praying and requests for prayer.** Paul prays for inner growth. *For this cause I bow my knees unto the Father of our Lord Jesus Christ, of whom the whole family in heaven and earth is named, that he would grant you according to the riches of his glory, to be strengthened with might by his Spirit in the inner man; that Christ may dwell in your hearts by faith; that ye, being rooted and grounded in love, may be able to comprehend with all saints what is the breadth, and length, and dept, and height; and to know the love of Christ, which passeth knowledge that ye might be filled with all the fullness of God (Ephesians 3:14-19)*.....Paul prayed three times about the thorn in his flesh.

*And when he had thus spoken, he kneeled down, and prayed with them all (Acts 20:36). And it came to pass, that the father of Publius lay sick of a fever and of a bloody flux: to whom Paul entered in, and prayed, and laid his hands on him, and healed him (Acts 28:8).*

When the apostle Paul was in Rome waiting to be trial he wrote to the Philippians. His prayer here in Philippians 1:9, 9-11) begins with an appeal that these believers' love may abound. The word "abound" used here means "overflowing" or more than enough – enough for their families, friends, enemies and also enough to extend to the lost and dying world around them.

Paul made it clear to them that he was suggesting an intelligent love – praying that they would grow in love while increasing in knowledge and judgment. He prayed for the kind of knowledgeable love that would give them the ability to distinguish between good and evil.

Paul prayed that they (the Philippians) might not only distinguish between good and evil by their sound judgment, but that they would be empowered to choose the best course in every situation. He then prayed that they would be sincere, without offense, and filled with the fruits of righteousness. These are all moral qualities that would enable them to live a life that would glorify God.

Paul recognized that the fruits of righteousness, which are in right standing with God as well as righteous deeds, are through Christ alone and not by man's efforts. The cry of his heart was that he desired to be found in Christ – not having mine own righteousness, which is of the law, but that which is through the faith of Christ, the righteousness which is of God by faith: (Philippians 3:9). The work of the Spirit in our life is not automatic. The gifts and fruit of the Spirit and God's power and anointing are manifested in our life as we pray.

Therefor it is very important that we learn to pray for the needs of those who are out of work, sick, or facing difficult times. The most important prayers that we can offer for others are rooted in God's priorities for them as believers as illustrated by this prayer.

**Paul and Barnabas** – *And when they had fasted and prayed, and laid their hands on them, they sent them away (Acts 13:3).*

**Paul and Silas (How to pray in the midnight hour)?** Paul and Silas wanted to go to Asia, but Acts 16:6 says they were forbidden of the Holy Ghost to preach the word in Asia. Then they tried to go to Bithynia, but Acts 16:7 says; *the Spirit suffered them not.*

God was supernaturally controlling their destinies. In Acts 16:8-9 we read that they went to Troas and Paul had a vision. A man of Macedonia appeared and pleaded with him, saying, come over into Macedonia, and help us. So Paul went to Philippi, a colony in Macedonia.

On the Sabbath, we find Paul and Silas out by a river speaking to a few women who opened their hearts to the Word (Acts 16:13-16). Perhaps they would have been thinking; if I could have just gone to Asia, I could have reached so many more. Here, I am with a few ladies by a river – not even speaking in a church, just having a little prayer meeting, only a few people getting saved; but God had a plan. Empowered by the prayer meeting, Paul and Silas began to move around the city of Philippi, ministering the Gospel. As long as you keep a low profile, Satan isn't all that concerned. When you begin to move in the power of the Spirit, you had better watch out!

A demon possessed girl began creating a disruption wherever they went. Finally, Paul dealt with this annoyance by casting the spirit out of her. That is the way to deal with annoying circumstances. Instead of trying to wish them away, manipulate, or psychoanalyze them, deal with them in the power of the Name of Jesus.

Paul's actions angered the girl's masters because they were using her for income from fortune telling. They incited a riot, made false accusations, and Paul and Silas were beaten and thrown in prison, with their feet fastened in stocks.

There are two things in this story that are common to us all. First, everyone faces prisons: prisons of circumstances, a difficult job, sinful habits, and physical or mental bondage. Second, everyone faces the "Midnights" of life. Night represents darkness, trials, and tests. When you stand by that open grave of a loved one, it's midnight. When your business fails, and you lose everything, it's midnight. When your friends turn their back on you; your marriage falls apart, or you have lost everything, it's midnight.

Now, my question is; can you trust God in your prison of circumstances? What will you do in your midnight hour? Paul and Silas sang praises; and at midnight Paul and Silas prayed, and sang praises unto God, and the prisoners heard them. And suddenly there was a great earthquake, so that the foundations of the prison were shaken: and immediately all the doors were opened, and every one's bands were loosed (Acts 16:25-26). In response to the prayers of Paul and Silas, God sent an earthquake, shook the foundations of the prison, opened the prison doors, and chains were broken.

Remember that Paul and Silas were in Philippi by God's design. He had a purpose. He has a purpose in the prison experiences and the midnight hours of your life, also. As Paul and Silas worshipped God, an earthquake occurred, chains were loosed, and the prison doors opened. This led to the conversion of the Philippian jailer, his entire household, and the establishment of a thriving church at Philippi.

When you praise God at midnight in the depths of you prison, five things happen: (1) **Receptivity:** People around you notice. The prisoners heard them. They became receptive to Paul and Silas. (2) **Rectify:** God takes notice. If necessary, a spiritual earthquake will occur to rectify and set right your circumstances. (3) **Release:** People lives are changed – chains are loosed, and prison doors are opened. (4) **Reverse:** The plan of the enemy will be reversed. Often, God will touch the very ones who have been the keeper of your prison, as in this account. The Philippian jailer was saved and ministered to Paul and Silas. (5) **Ripple:** A divine ripple effect occurs as the miracle in the midnight hour spreads to touch the lives of others. The entire household of the Philippian jailer was saved.

Are you in prison? Is it midnight in your life? Are you bound by the prison of sin or negative circumstances? Your past habits? If you will praise Him in the midst of your prison, in the midnight of your life, you will receive your miracle.

**According to the biblical records, God walked into personal prisons and:** Joseph was raised to be the leader of the land. Samson's hair began to grow, and he conquered more of the enemy in his death than in his life. Imprisoned prophets birthed revelations that extended to our day. Jeremiah bought a field by faith, knowing that someday deliverance would come. Daniel was elevated from the lion's den to leadership. John, imprisoned on Patmos, saw the greatest vision of all time while he was in the Spirit on the Lord's Day (Revelation 1:10) – not griping and complaining or trying to build a raft to get off of the Island.

**You are not alone in the prisons of your life.** Paul said: *At my first defense no one stood with me, but all forsook me. May it not be charged against them? But the Lord stood with me and strengthened me, so that the message might be preached fully through me. And that all the Gentiles might hear. Also I was delivered out of the mouth of the lion. And the Lord will* *deliver me from every evil work and preserve me for His heavenly kingdom. To Him be the glory forever and ever. Amen! (2Timothy 4:16-18 NKJV)*

The Lord stands with you in your midnight hour, in the prisons of your life. Begin to praise Him, and you will see things change.

**Peter** – *But Peter put them all forth, and kneeled down, and prayed; and turning him to the body said, Tabitha, arise. And she opened her eyes; and when she saw Peter, she sat up (Acts 9:40). And on the morrow, as they went on their journey, and drew nigh unto the city, Peter went up upon the housetop to pray about the sixth hour (Acts 10:9). But Peter put them all forth, and kneeled down, and prayed; and turning him to the body said, Tabitha, arise. And she opened her eyes; and when she saw Peter, she sat up (Acts 9:40).*

**Peter and John – Prayer in the face of persecution:** Following the coming of the Holy Spirit, the apostles gave a powerful witness to the Gospel. In Acts Chapter 3, on the way to prayer at the temple, Peter and John encountered a lame man and, using their delegated authority of the Name of Jesus, commanded him to rise up and walk.

On the following day the high priests confronted Peter, John, and the man who had been healed. They asked the disciples, by what power, or by what name, have ye done this (Acts 4:7)? Peter, now full of the Holy Ghost, was not intimidated, as he had been at the time of the crucifixion, when he had denied Christ. The Holy Ghost prayer meeting in the Upper Room had changed his life. Peter boldly declared: *Be it known unto you all, and to all the people of Israel, that by the name of Jesus*

*Christ of Nazareth, whom ye crucified, whom God raised from the dead, even by him doth this man stand here before you whole (Acts 4:10).*

Peter clearly explained to them that it is by the power and authority of Jesus' name that this man is healed. You crucified Him, but He is not in the grave. God raised Him from the dead, and He is sitting at the right hand of the Father. He has delegated to us power and authority in His Name, and it is by His name that this man is healed.

Peter did not stop there; he made it clear that there is no other name whereby men can be saved. He said, *neither is there salvation in any other: for there is none other name under heaven given among men, whereby we must be saved (Acts 4:12).*

We need the same power and boldness in the church today. Instead of compromising and trying to be politically correct, we must boldly proclaim that there is no other name – not Buddha, not Mohammed, not any of the Hindu gods, whereby men can be saved! There is only one way to God, and only one name – the name of Jesus Christ the Son of the living God.

After the high priests threatened Peter and John and warned them not to preach or teach in Jesus' Name, they released them. But Peter and John did not retreat to hide in safety, have a pity party, or devise a plan to win over the high priests. They met with the other believers and had a prayer meeting. They did not ask God to stop the persecution but prayed intensely, with great fervency, and in one accord.

*And, now, Lord, behold their threatening: and grant unto thy servants, that with all boldness they may speak thy word, by stretching forth thine hand to heal; and that signs and wonders may be done by the name of thy holy child Jesus (Acts 4:29-30).* Their prayer was not focused on the power of the enemy. They did not ask God to change the heart of the high priests and religious leaders. Their prayer was specific. They only ask for two things: 1. Boldness – boldness to speak the Word and 2. Signs and wonders to be done in Jesus' Name. God heard their prayer and sent a spiritual earthquake. *And when they had prayed, the place was shaken where they were assembled together, and they were all filled with the Holy Ghost, and they spake the Word of God with boldness (Acts 4:31).*

The disciples left the prayer meeting charged with the Power of God. They refused to be intimidated and continued to boldly proclaim the Gospel and work signs and wonders in the name of Jesus. *And daily in the temple, and in every house, they ceased not to teach and preach Jesus Christ (Acts 5:42).* The results of their prayer was boldness, unity of purpose, and beauty of character when grace was upon them all (Acts 4:33).

The believers flooded Jerusalem with the Gospel, and multitudes were added to the Church. The power of God was so greatly manifested that people carried the sick and placed them on cots along the street so that as Peter passed by, his shadow might fall on them, and they would be healed. *There came also a multitude out of the cities round about unto Jerusalem, bringing sick folks, and them which were vexed with unclean spirits; and they were healed every one (Acts 5:16).*

From this response to persecution, we learn that when threats come, get with the people of God and pray. Confess the greatness of God to strengthen your faith. Don't complain or retreat, but pray for new doors of effective ministry to open, that you will be filled with the Holy Spirit, and that God will confirm His Word with signs following.

Now when the apostles who were at Jerusalem heard that Samaria had received the Word of God, they sent unto them Peter and John: *Who, when they were come down, prayed for them, that they might receive the Holy Ghost (Acts 8:15).*

**Pharisee** – *The Pharisee stood and prayed thus with himself, God I thank thee, that I am not as other men are, exhortioner, unjust, adulterers, or even as this publican (Luke 18:11).*

**Stephen** (Dying Prayer). Stephen was the first martyr who gave a powerful and convicting witness to the Gospel. The authorities were infuriated at his words, dragged him outside the city, and stoned him to death. Thus, Stephen became the first Christian martyr.

As Stephen was dying amidst the pelting stones, he was calling on God, saying, *Lord Jesus, receive my spirit (Acts 7:59). And he kneeled down, and cried with a loud voice, Lord; lay not this sin to their charge. And when he had said this, he fell asleep (Acts 7:60).*

Stephen didn't pray for deliverance or a miracle to affect his release. Sometimes, the Will of God is accomplished in dying as much as in living. In Hebrews, Chapter 11, we have the record of some great people who were delivered and others who were martyred. All of them are referred to as men and women of faith.

Whenever we find it difficult to forgive someone, we should recall Stephen's dying prayer. In the midst of his pain and suffering, he forgave. While they were killing him, he pleaded on their behalf and asked that their sins be forgiven. Stephen maintained the spirit of forgiveness that Jesus had modeled and taught.

**The Apostles** – *And when they heard that, they lifted up their voice to God with one accord, and said, Lord, thou art God, which hast made heaven and earth, and the sea and all that in them is (Acts 4:24). Whom they set before the apostles, and when they had prayed, they laid their hands on them (Luke 6:6).*

**The Dying Thief** – *And he said unto Jesus, Lord, remember me when thou comest into thy kingdom (Luke 23:42).*

**The Early Church (true prayers heard).** *Because they turned back from him, and would not consider any of his ways: So that they cause the cry of the poor to come unto him, and he heareth the cry of the afflicted (Job 34:27-28).*

*And when they had prayed the place was shaken where they were assembled together and they were all filled with the Holy Ghost, and they spake the Word of God with boldness (Act 4:31).*

*Peter therefore was kept in prison, but prayer was made without ceasing of the church unto God for him (James 5:16).*

**The Publican** – *And the publican, standing afar off, would not lift up so much as his eyes unto heaven, but smote upon his breast, saying, God be merciful to me a sinner (Luke 18:13).* The heart was regarded as the seat of sin. The Publican's action implies acute contrition and a sense of personal unworthiness. To obtain forgiveness he thinks not of his own works but solely of God's mercy.

**The Syrophenician Woman** – *And behold, a woman of Canaan came out of the same coasts, and cried unto him saying, Have mercy on me, O Lord, thou Son of David; my daughter is grievously vexed with a devil. Then came she and worshipped him saying, Lord, help me (Matthew 15:22, 25).*

**The ten Lepers:** *And as he entered into a certain village, there met him ten men that were lepers, which stood afar off: And they lifted up their voices, and said, Jesus, Master, have mercy on us (Luke 17:12-13).*

**Zechariah's:** *But the angel said unto him, Fear not, Zacharias; for thy prayer is heard, and thy wife Elisabeth shall bear thee a son, and thou shalt call his name John (Luke 1:13).*

### Jabezs' Prayer (1 Chronicles 4:9-10)

*And Jabez was more honourable than his brethren; and his mother called his name Jabez, saying, because I bare him with sorrow. And Jabez called on the God of Israel, saying, Oh that thou wouldest bless me indeed, and enlarge my coast, and that thine hand might be with me, and that thou wouldest keep me from evil, that it may not grieve me! And God granted him that which he requested.*

Now the Hebrew word here for honorable has both a positive and negative meaning. In the positive sense, it means "rich, abounding, and noble." The negative means "grievously afflicted, sore and dim." So which meaning fits the man, Jabez: Given his name and the kind of prayer he prayed, the negative meaning of the word honorable is the one that most adequately describes Jabez. At birth, this young man was given a name which interpreted means "sorrow, distress, grief, and pain." In the Bible days, names were significant, so from the day Jabez was born he was marked as a sorrowful painful person.

Jabezs' prayer, although brief, is one of the most significant in the Old Testament record. Here is a man who all his life lived on the downside, sorrowful, lonely, heartsick, shunned by others, poor, in need, perhaps even dim-witted – but one day he called on the God of Israel for a blessing. When you call on God in faith, something will happen. Forget about your sorrow and grief. Forget about your mental capacity or how others view you. Jabez could have settled for a life of sorrow and pain, reflecting the meaning of his name, but he didn't. Instead, he called upon the God of Israel for a blessing.

His prayer was not filled with the usual fluff, froth, flowery words, and repetitious phrases to which we have become accustomed. It was simple, straightforward, and to the point. *Oh that you would bless me indeed! (1 Chronicle 4:10).* This was not a selfish prayer, because it is only when you are blessed and not weighed down by your own issues that you can be a blessing to others. God is seeking those who will dare to pray in simplicity and in faith, those who will not be afraid to say with Jabez, bless me! Jabez asked God to enlarge his coast. The Hebrew word for enlarge is rabah, which means "increase, abundance, authority, excel, be full, great gather, take in, multiply, nourish, have plenty." This word reflects the unfathomable faith of Jabez's heart. He was daring to become what he had not been, to dream big. He was breaking the mold, shattering the bounds, destroying the yoke, cutting the cords and stepping out on a new uncharted path. His prayer was not; Give me strength to endure one more day, it was... enlarge my coast...

The second word in this portion of Jabez's prayer in Hebrew is *ghebool*. Eight different words are used to fully describe this word; "territory, boundary, landmark, border, coast, limit, quarter, and space," Jabez was saying to God: I want you to extend my territory; take off the limits. The space where I am living is too small. Enlarge the borders of my thinking, my faith, my living, and my giving! Jabez no longer wanted to settle for just getting by and living the settled life.

Next, Jabez asked...*that thine hand might be with me...*Jabez was asking for a close, one-on-one relationship, akin to that which patriarchs Abraham, Isaac, and Jacob had with God. This request also referenced the blessing of fathers upon sons, as illustrated by Abraham blessing Isaac, Isaac blessing Jacob, and Jacob blessing the sons of joseph. Jabez saw the hand of God as a mighty weapon and a conquering force (Psalms 44:1-3). He saw it as protection in times of trouble (Psalms 138:7). He saw it as a source of deliverance (Psalms 60:4-5) and provision (Psalms 145:16). With His hand upon us we are preserved, protected, sheltered, and shielded from the onslaughts of the enemy. His hand makes us impregnable. Then Jabez declared; ...*and that thou wouldest keep me from evil, that it may not grieve me...*

Now there are four distinct areas we need God to guard in order to keep us from evil and keep us from being grieved by the enemy.

The first area is in our spirit. The greatest battles we fight are in the spirit. We do not wrestle against flesh and blood, but against principalities, powers, rulers of darkness, and spiritual wickedness (Ephesians 6:12; 2 Corinthians 10:4).

The second area is in our mind. The world is filled with opinions, beliefs, and concepts contrary to the Word of God. Satan would fill your mind with fear and unbelief. Ask God to renew your mind each day as you reflect on His Word (2Corinthians 4:16).

The third area is the words we speak. *For by your words you will be justified, and by your words you will be condemned (Matthew 12:37, NKJV).* Your words are powerful for both good and evil. That's why it is so important that you learn to confess and speak only that which blesses and edifies the hearer, including yourself, because you – more than anyone else, hears the things you say.

The fourth area is in our finances. Every child of God must guard their finances with prayer and vigilance, lest they violate the principles set forth in both the Old and New Testaments. God's command to us is, *Always remember that it is the Lord your God who gives you power to become rich, and he does it to fulfill his promise to your ancestors (Deuteronomy 8:18, TLB).* God entrusts riches into our hands so we can enjoy life, but we are also entrusted with wealth so that we can help the poor and advance the work of the Kingdom of God.

The concluding phrase of Jabez's prayer is, And God granted him that which he requested. Turn to Deuteronomy, Chapter 29, and read through the extended list of the promises of God. These blessings are not reserved for heaven. God wants to bless you now. Claim them in prayer, and God will grant that which you request.

You must repeat this fantastic little prayer each day during your devotions. Let these words find lodging in your spirit. Let them flow from your heart as you seek the face of God in your times of intercession, and the God who answered the cry of Jabez will also answer you.

# The Prayers of the Saints (The Children of God) Availeth much

Now let's take a look at the eighth Chapter of Revelation. Lit talks about what the Children of God done when the seventh seal were open. When Christ opens the seventh seal, there was silence in heaven about the space of half an hour. There were no earthquakes, no thundering, no lightening, no voices, no praise and worship, just total silence according to Revelation, Chapter 8. For a period of about a half hour there was a breathless silence, as God prepared to pour out His judgments upon the earth.

At some point during this profound silence, seven angels assemble before God, and each of them are given a trumpet. Then another angel comes and stands at the altar, having a golden censer and incense, symbolizing the prayers of the saints. Now, many times the word angel is used for a man, since it means "messenger." Other times it is used for the angels in heaven. Revelation 8:3 says, *and another angel came and stood at the altar to minister.* This would seem to indicate that the angel is Christ in His present ministry as our high priest – *even*

*Jesus, made an High Priest for ever after the order of Melchisedec (Hebrews 6:20). We notice that the censer is always mentioned in connection with the high priest (Leviticus 16:12).*

A censer was a dish or shallow bowl that hung by a chain or was carried with tongs. Inside the censer were placed incense (s combination of sweet-smelling spices) and live coals from the altar. And on the Day of Atonement, the High Priest entered the most Holy Place carrying a smoking censer. The smoke shielded him from the Ark of the Covenant and the presence of God. Otherwise he would die. Incense may also have had a very practical purpose here. The reason I'm saying this is because, the sweet smell drew the people's attention to the morning and evening sacrifices and helped to comer their sometimes foul smell.

As the prayers of the saints ascend before God, filling heaven with a sweet smelling aroma, the angel fills the censer with fire from the altar and casts it down upon the earth (Revelation 8:4-5). Then suddenly the silence in heaven is shattered. Voices sound, lightning flashes, thunder crashes, the earth shakes, and the seven angels prepared to sound their trumpets.

Therefore, I feel it is very important that we understand the tremendous significance of the prayers of God's people and how prayer is vitally linked with God's end-time plan. In these verses – right before God's judgments are poured out upon the wicked, the prayers of God's people are offered to God on the golden altar before His throne. The prayer ascends unto God, along with the incense, and becomes a sweet-smelling savor in His nostrils.

Now let us take a look at what happen before Christ opened the seven seals in Revelation, Chapter 5. The elders and cherubim also lifted up golden vials full of odors, symbolizing the prayers of the saints. In both of these crucial moments in the unfolding of God's end-time plan, the prayers of God's people ascended before His throne and activated the process.

Our prayers here on Earth on behalf of the lost, our cries to God regarding the wickedness and immorality surrounding us, our intercession for God's intervention against the evil forces unleashed on the world today, are not forgotten. They ascend before God as sweet-smelling incense in His nostrils.

In response to these prayers of the saints, the angel (Jesus Christ) takes the censer, fills it with fire, and casts it down to the Earth. The prayers of God's people release the seven angels to sound their trumpets, which unleash the judgments of God upon the wicked.

Right now, throughout the world, God is pouring out the last great anointing, which is the end-time prayer. He is bringing us to a new strategic level of warfare prayer. Through this strategic level of prayer, the people of God will be used mightily in this end time to push back the enemy in the nations, to tear down the strongholds blinding the hearts and minds of the lost, and to release those who are bound by Satan's power.

God has given us His Church, and His Power of Attorney. We are His delegated authority upon the Earth. As we enter into this new level of warfare prayer, and begin to pray with authority, God will release His power to fulfill His end-time plan. In response to the prayers of God's people, we will see the greatest demonstration in history of His mighty power, His miracles, His healing, His deliverance, and His restoration greater than we have ever known or though.

# The Lord's Prayer/
# The Disciples Prayer
## A sermon by: Rev. Fred Cato, Jr.

Many people today are abusing the Lord's Prayer, but here Jesus is giving instruction in the Sermon on the Mount, warning us against the acts to be seen of men. He is warning us against the hypocritical manner of prayer, such as praying in the synagogue and on the street corners to be seen of men. He teaches us that man ought to pray in the closet with the doors closed. With the door closed, you will not be tempted to show off. The closed door shuts out everything else so that you can concentrate on God, and pray to your Father which is in heaven, that God may enter the closet making a way for a relationship that cannot be broken by the things on the outside.

The closed door is the wall between the carnal and the spiritual. It is the difference between the curse and the blessings; and the divider between acceptance and redemption. Therefore, when you pray, if you will go into your closet, He will reward you openly; that the world may know that there must be a God somewhere.

There is one thing we don't want, and that is the reputation of the heathens, who prays to insult the wisdom of God. They make mockery of the knowledge of Tod and make Him seem incapable of keeping His promise. God can hear you when you pray. God is even able to hear your whisper. He can hear your faintest cry; and He will answer in due time.

Jesus concludes by giving a guide to prayer by saying: "After this manner therefore pray ye; Our Father". Many are puzzled as to what prayer really is. Prayer is communion with God, and if God is not involved, then, there is only a pretense of prayer. Not only must He be involved, but centrally involved. Prayer is God's provision: It is God's idea, not man. There could be no prayer if God did not condescend to speak with us, and we could not know how to pray had He not chosen to instruct us. When our prayer is as it should be, Our Father who sees in secret will repay us. The most important secret He sees is not the words we say in the privacy of our room, but the thought we have in the privacy of our heart.

The purpose of prayer is not to inform or persuade God, but to come before Him sincerely, purposely, consciously, and devotedly. Prayer is sharing the needs, burdens, and hunger of our hearts before our heavenly Father, who already knows what we need, but who wants us to ask Him. He wants to hear us. He wants to commune with us, more that we could ever want to commune with Him, because His love for us is so much greater than our love for Him. Prayer is our giving God the opportunity to manifest His power, majesty, love, and providence.

To pray rightly is to pray with a devout heart and with pure motives. It is to pray with single attention to God rather than to other men. And it is to pray with sincere confidence that our Heavenly Father both hears and answers every request made to Him in faith. He always repays our sincere devotion with gracious response. If our request is sincere, but not according to His will, He will answer in a way better than we want or expect. But He will always answer.

The dictionary defines prayer as the act of soliciting an honest request. Some says it is a sincere desire of the heart; but it is prayer that makes every believer in Christ real. Prayer seems to be the relationship between father and child. Prayer strengthens the faith that believes God is. *Hebrews 11:6 says; He that comest to God must believe that He is, and that He is a rewarder of them that diligently seek Him.* Prayer forms the mysterious clouds by day and a pillar of fire by night. Prayer is the pathway that leadeth us to the Throne of God. Prayer is so amplified that God hears it before the words are ended.

It does not matter what position you are in, God will hear you. You may kneel or you may stand. It does not matter how long or how short you prayer is; your prayers may be brief such as Lord save me, or Lord have mercy on me, or you prayer may be of many words. It may be as the prayer of Solomon, where God told Solomon, that because he asked for wisdom, and had not asked for the life of his enemies, the Lord did according to Solomon's request.

Now let's take another look at the Lord's Prayer, it says, "After this manner, therefore pray ye". Now it took only 66 words to complete the greatest prayer ever uttered; 66 words without saying the same thing twice. So as we can see God is a just God; His dwelling place is recognized; His guidance is suggested, and His protection is admitted. These 66 words match the books of the Bible. It took Solomon, the wise man more than 140 words to complete his desire; but there is a man wiser than Solomon, and that man name is Jesus, who gave us 66 words in order to reach the needs of the Children of God.

**"Our Father, which art in Heaven"** He's all universal; Our Father, all loving and all powerful. Many parents die and go into judgment without ever holding their little gifts in their arms, without even kissing that little son or daughter. Our Father; He knows all of us as His children, and He will not put on us a burden that's too hard to bear. When your load gets heavy, you can always go to the Father, because; Our Father which art in heaven is the one we should give all the glory, honors, and praise to. We need to acknowledge His residence, which is in heaven, from whence cometh all our blessings. Our Father; He's so far away and yet He's so close. When you're in danger or trouble, you can look up and say: "Father! I'm in your care, and I want you to put your loving arms around me, that no evil on earth can harm me.

**"Hallowed be thy name".** The name of Our Father makes Him different from all other beings. That is why I get disturb when I hear someone taking the name of the Lord in vain. His name implies strength. He's the beginning and the end; He's the first and the last. He doesn't need anyone to do anything for Him; He can do it all by Himself. He can bring to pass whatever He will. He does not have to swear by heaven or by earth. He can swear by Himself, placing His right hands upon His thigh and declaring I am God and beside me, there is no other, and what He commands will stand. I don't care how old or how young you are; I don't care how strong or how healthy you are; you cannot make it alone. You need the Lord on your journey. You need Him to walk and talk with you. You cannot travel this road alone; you need to take the Lord along with you. There is something about His name that I love to hear – it smooths my doubt and calms my fears.

**"Thy Kingdom come"** (the fast universe). In the beginning God created the heaven and the earth. Here, we can see that all things are subject to His command. He is King and He is Lord. Let your kingdom come within us. Everyone should be able to say, well Lord, since you are King, you can rule; rule in my heart, rule in my life, speak, and take control; let your kingdom come within me.

**"Thy will be done in earth as it is in heaven."** At His command the sun shines; at His command the moon rules the night; at His command the stars reflect; at His command the wind blows, at His command the lightning flashes; at His command the thunder roars; at His command the water rises and falls; at His command the earth brings forth.

**"Give us this day, our daily bread."** You ought to tell the Lord that all you need is your daily bread; to know that you are in fellowship with God; to know that He'll fight your battle and that He'll build a fence around you, that Satan tempts you not. Nobody can do this but God. I'm not worry, when I can tell my Lord and Savior to feed me. Give me enough of food daily. I'm not going to fret about it. Give me my daily bread.

**"And forgive us our debts, as we forgive our debtors."** Now here I think each of us is in debt to God for something. But do we really know what it means to be in debt: Most of us have valuables – we purchased them on an installment plan. We pay a little this month and a little next month, and sometimes we miss paying and we know what the consequences are. What I am trying to say is that we are in debt to God. Therefore, we must ask the Lord to forgive us our debts. We owe the Lord something; and I feel we all should try paying God a little on our debts. When we wake up in the morning we should say, "Lord, I just want to make a little installment on my debts by saying; "thank your Jesus, for my lying down on last night – thank you for my uprising this morning; "Thank you for keeping me closed in my right mind." He's worthy; He's worthy of all praises; and that is why we ought to praise Him at all times as the scripture said in 1 Thessalonians 5:17, "Pray without ceasing," meaning to continue in prayer and never cease from praying.

**"And lead us not into temptation."** I'm tempted to sleep; I'm tempted to be at ease; I'm tempted to give up when I should go on, because I can't receive my crown until I have reached the end of my journey.

**"But deliver us from evil."** One evil is persecution. **For thine is the Kingdom, and the power, and the glory, forever, A-men."** Now when Paul and Silas were in prison, they must have said A-men, because when the clock reached the midnight hour, I don't know what they said, but they must have said: "Father! I stretch my hand to thee – no other help I know." Father! I'm in Your care, and I'm going to leave it in Your hands; You can fix it; You can take full control, and You can make man leave me alone.

**In conclusion:** Don't take your problems upon yourself: Take them to the Lord in prayer. Prayer changes things.

# *Author's Note*

 Many times, when we are facing difficult situations, we do not know exactly how we should pray, but thank God for the Holy Ghost who comes to our rescue (aid). God's Spirit prays through us. With this divine help from the Holy Spirit, we can intercede even when we don't know what or how to pray. Sometimes the Holy Spirit intercedes through us in our native language by giving wisdom as to how to pray. Other times, the Holy Spirit prays through us in our prayer language. Sometimes prayer is just simply a groan that words cannot express.

Prayer changes things – and one of the greatest changes, is the change in the one that's praying. Prayer will change your attitude - it will change your disposition – It will change the way you see things – it will change the way you talk – It will change the way you dress – it will change the way you act – it will change the way you live your life – it will turn your life around 180 degrees. Moreover, it will make you become a new creature. Prayer is the key to God's kingdom.

# *Bibliography*

**Evang. Fred Cato Jr.** - Words of Inspiration, Morris Publishing Company, Kearney, NE 1996.

**Evang. Fred Cato Jr.** - Feed the Children, Author House Publishing Co. Bloomington, IN 2006.

**Evang. Fred Cato Jr.** - Mr. Lowdown and his Principles, Author House Pub. Co. Bloomington, IN 2006.

**Min. Fred Cato, Jr.** - **Poems** of Inspiration, Xlibris Publishing Co. Bloomington, IN 2007

Printed in the United States
by Baker & Taylor Publisher Services